PL 1:
A Structured
Approach

Don Cassel

Reston Publishing Company, Inc.
A Prentice-Hall Company
Reston, Virginia 22090

Library of Congress Cataloging in Publication Data

Cassel, Don
    Programming language one.

    Includes index.
    1. PL/1 (Computer program language) I. Title.
HF5548.5.P2C36 1978   001.6'425   77-16809
ISBN 0-87909-650-0

10 9 8 7 6 5 4 3 2 1

Printed in the United States of America.

To Pamela

Contents

Preface

Since my book *Programming Language One* was published in 1972, several significant changes have occurred in the programming field. The first and foremost of these has been the widespread adoption of structured programming concepts. This approach to program design, coding, and debugging is a very effective procedure for producing programs which are relatively error free, easy to read, and easy to debug.

PL/I is a particularly good language for teaching structured programming. The three basic control structures—Sequence, If-Then-Else and Do While—are all directly available in PL/I. This allows the concepts of structured programming to be taught without conflict between theory and practice. In some languages this is not possible. Go To less programming is also feasible in PL/I and is an ideal way for the beginner to learn logic development. Although Go To's may occasionally be effective, they have been avoided in the programs used in this text.

A second consideration in writing this book was the increased use of PL/C by the educator. PL/C offers an excellent introduction to programming in PL/I. PL/C programs also compile and execute considerably faster than traditional compilers. This is particularly valuable for the educational institute where there is a high volume of student compiles. All programs in the first eight chapters have been compiled and tested with PL/C.

The book assumes no prior knowledge of programming. The student begins with a basic introduction to the language and progresses gradually to the more complex areas of PL/I. Initially sample programs are of an elementary nature and are basically intended to expose the student to the fundamentals of

PL/I. As new areas of the language are discussed, additional programs are included to demonstrate their application.

Programming assignments also begin at a relatively simple level and progress through various stages of difficulty. There are 56 programming assignments in the book which should provide adequate flexibility for most courses. These assignments cover a broad spectrum including payroll, sales, banking, job reporting, tax, inventory control, insurance, production, education, depreciation, purchasing and numerous general interest programs to develop problem solving ability.

Chapters 1 to 7 inclusive are essential to every course in PL/I. For those students who have studied Fortran there are many similarities between the two languages. Thus Chapter 4, on arithmetic expressions, may be discussed rather quickly if a student has had this background. If the course is a short one, or not intended to be in-depth, then these chapters may be sufficient.

However, the more advanced or in-depth course will probably use the entire book. For a well-rounded business-oriented course, Chapters 9 and 10 are important since they deal with record oriented file processing, which is an integral part of business data processing. It is important for the student to get some actual programming experience on file updating techniques. This ensures his understanding of the language and serves as an introduction to the concept of programming in large business systems.

Finally, I would like to express appreciation to those whose contributions helped to produce this book. To my wife who did much of the typing, my students who taught me a lot, and my colleagues who gave many excellent suggestions.

Don Cassel

Introduction to PL/I

PL/I is one of the many high-level programming languages used for communicating with computers. It was developed by International Business Machines Corporation for use with their System/360 series of computers. The abbreviation PL/I comes from the name: Programming Language One.

The use of a high-level language such as PL/I permits the programmer to instruct the computer in such operations as addition, subtraction, multiplication, division, and exponentiation without a detailed knowledge of the inner workings of the computer. However, our study of this language will provide a foundation for further studies in programming in lower-level languages (Assembler, for example).

Basic operations which are unique to computers are retained in this language. These operations are the ability to make decisions and the ability to store instructions in some storage medium. There is nothing mystical about these abilities since the computer is in reality responding to commands given to it by a human programmer who made these decisions when writing the program. The usefulness of a computer revolves around the speed with which it carries out these operations and particularly its ability to change the type of computation it is doing through decision-making processes. These decisions must have first been made by the PL/I programmer and then communicated to the computer by means of the PL/I language. Decisions will be discussed in detail in Chapter 6.

Procedures

All PL/I programs consist of at least one procedure which contains the statements needed for the program. Figure 1-1 shows a sample PL/I program which consists of one main procedure called SAMPLE.

```
01  SAMPLE:PROCEDURE OPTIONS(MAIN);
02      DECLARE NUM DECIMAL FIXED(5),
03          HOURS DECIMAL FIXED(3),
04          RATE DECIMAL FIXED(5,2),
05          PAY DECIMAL FIXED(7,2);
06      GET LIST(NUM,HOURS,RATE);
07      PAY=HOURS*RATE;
08      PUT LIST(NUM,HOURS,RATE,PAY);
09      STOP;
10      END;
```

Fig. 1-1 *A Sample PL/I Program*

This example shows a number of items common to most PL/I programs. Initially the program must begin with a Procedure statement similar to the one shown on line 01 of the sample. The general format to be used when writing a Procedure statement is shown in Fig. 1-2.

Fig. 1-2

label	A name consisting of 1 to 6 characters in length. A maximum of seven is acceptable in the F-level compiler. This is the name which identifies the procedure. It must always begin with an alphabetic character followed by alphabetic or numeric characters.
:	A colon always follows a label.
PRØCEDURE	Identifies this statement as being the first statement of the program. The word Procedure is known as a Keyword. (See Appendix A)

ØPTIØNS(MAIN)   Identifies this as being the main procedure.

;   A semicolon ,always terminates a statement in PL/I.

Each procedure statement begins with a label which identifies the procedure. In our example we called this procedure SAMPLE. It is usual to choose a name which in some way describes the type of program to be written. Therefore, instead of SAMPLE we could have chosen the name PAYROL since this is a payroll program. It does not matter that the final L is dropped from this name since we can use any abbreviations desired for label names. In fact the word PAYRØLL could not be used by the D compiler since it exceeds 6 characters in length.

The PL/I procedure in Fig. 1–1 is terminated by an END statement. Every PL/I procedure requires an END. The general format for an END is shown in Fig. 1–3.

---

1 2

END [*label*] ;

Fig. 1–3

END   Keyword which identifies the type of statement.

[*label*]   The brackets indicate this label is optional. If the label is used it would be the name of the procedure which it is terminating; i.e., END SAMPLE;

;   A semicolon terminates the statement.

Contained within the procedure of Fig. 1–1 we have additional statements which are the program itself.

Lines 02 to 05 are Declares which reserve storage space for items to be read from data cards or items to be calculated. Declares will be considered in detail in Chapter 3.

Line 06 causes data to be read from an input device, such as a card reader, into the variables named NUM, HØURS, and RATE. These are symbolic names for reserved storage areas which have been previously declared.

Line 07 is an arithmetic statement which causes HØURS to be multiplied by RATE. The result of this calculation will be stored in a location called PAY.

Line 08 tells the computer we wish to print the result of our calculation along with the original input data.

Line 09 instructs the computer to stop the program since we have completed all necessary computations. This should not be confused with the END statement which is used to define the limits of the procedure.

Statements and Statement Labels

A PL/I program consists of basic elements called statements. There are simple statements and compound statements, each of which are terminated by a semicolon.

The statements used in the sample PL/I program are simple statements. In the case of the statement

GET LIST (NUM, HØURS,RATE);

the words GET and LIST are called Keywords. However, some simple statements do not contain a Keyword. An example of this is the statement

PAY = HØURS * RATE;

Here all of the names are names of variables which are to be used in the calculation.

A compound statement is one which contains one or more other statements. An IF statement is an example of a compound statement.

IF A>B THEN A = A+B;

The first part is the decision component IF A>B followed by the action component THEN A = A+B which is an arithmetic expression.

Statements may be preceded by a label to identify that statement thus permitting logical control of the program (see Chapter 6). The preceding examples might have been written as shown in Fig. 1-4.

---

1 | 2

READ: GET LIST (NUM,HØURS,RATE);
CALC: PAY = HØURS * RATE;
CØMPARE: IF A>B THEN A = A+B;

Fig. 1-4

A statement label can consist of up to 31 alphanumeric and break characters. This is not to be confused with a PRØCEDURE label which is restricted to 6 characters. The first character must be alphabetic. The following are examples of valid statement labels:

                    HØLD
                    UPDATE
                    MØVE_TØ_ØUTPUT
                    SWITCH5
                    MULTIPLY_A_B

The following labels are invalid:

        2HØLD
        SW A
        _MØVE
        5
        TAKE_INPUT_FIELD_AND_MØVE_IT_TØ_ØUTPUT

Statement labels are always followed with a colon as is shown in Fig. 1-4. This serves to separate the label from the statement.

Statements can begin anywhere between card columns 2 and 72 inclusive. There can be more than one statement per line and a statement may continue into the next line. Using this approach we could rewrite our sample program of Fig. 1-1 as shown in Fig. 1-5.

---

1 | 2

SAMPLE:PRØCEDURE ØPTIØNS(MAIN);
DECLARE NUM DECIMAL FIXED(5), HØURS DECIMAL FIXED(3),
RATE DECIMAL FIXED(5,2), PAY DECIMAL FIXED(7,2);
GET LIST(NUM,HØURS,RATE); PAY=HØURS*RATES; PUT
LIST(NUM,HØURS,RATE,PAY);STØP; END;

Fig. 1-5

Although this approach is more economical in terms of space used, it is much more difficult to read. In the event that an error is made when writing the program, the error is more difficult to find and correct in this program than in the first one. It is advisable to have only one statement per line. Organization such as that used in Fig. 1-1 will permit easier reading and debugging of the program.

Use of Blanks as Delimiters

At least one blank character must be used to separate entries in statements where no other character is used for separation. For example in the statement

GET LIST(NUM,HØURS,RATE);

a blank is used to separate or delimit the keywords GET and LIST. However, where a parenthesis or a comma is present, no blanks are required to separate words. Blanks may be used freely in the statement if desired. Thus we can get an equivalent statement by writing

---

GET LIST (NUM , HØURS , RATE);

The following characters when used in a PL/I program act as delimiters. Of course they have additional functions as we shall see later.

$$< \quad > \quad = \quad \neg$$
$$+ \quad - \quad * \quad /$$
$$(\quad) \quad | \quad \&$$
$$, \quad :$$

When any of these characters appear in a statement the use of blanks is not essential. This is demonstrated in the following examples.

N=J+K*(B−C);
IF N>L&A<B THEN NUM=SUM(1);
STORE='CHAR'||NAME;

Blanks cannot be used in identifiers or labels. The following show invalid use of blanks in a keyword and a label.

GET LIST
NUM

Comment Cards

Sometimes it is useful to include comments in the program to explain certain operations which may not be obvious to someone reading the program. It is important to be aware that comments in no way affect the operation of the program. They are for the benefit of the programmer, not the computer. The general format for comments is shown in Fig. 1-6.

1	2
	/* *comment* */

Fig. 1-6

The characters /* indicate the beginning of a comment and */ the end of the comment. Comments may be treated in a manner similar to statements in that they may use one or more lines or may occur between other statements. The PL/C compiler restricts comments to a single line. Thus, if a lengthy comment is required, several comment cards may be used. Some examples of comments are:

/* INVENTØRY UPDATE PRØGRAM */

/* THIS RØUTINE CALCULATES THE WEIGHTED AVERAGE
CØST FØR PRØDUCT CØDE 39 */

AVG=TØT/NUM; /* CALCULATE AVERAGE GRADE */

Source Program

The program which you as a PL/I programmer write is known as a source program. It is in a language which can be understood and used with relative ease compared to the computer's machine language. Since PL/I is not a machine language, a compiler must be used to translate the source program into a machine or object program.

The compiler reads the deck of cards which you have prepared after writing the PL/I program and translates each statement into equivalent machine language statements. While this is happening the compiler also produces a source listing which essentially is a printout of your PL/I program. If the program contains any errors, the compiler produces a list of these errors called diagnostics. The programmer must then correct these errors and recompile the program. See Fig. 1-7.

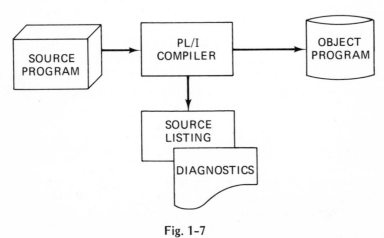

Fig. 1-7

Object Program

The program which the PL/I compiler produces as a result of its compilation is known as an object program. This program is in a language which the computer can now understand. After compilation, the object program is normally placed temporarily on a direct access device. In order for the object program to run it must be loaded into the Central Processing Unit (CPU). The instruction to do this is given by the Job Control Language (see page 9). Once the subject program has been loaded into storage, it is then executed. Data is read, computations are made, and output is produced. See Fig. 1-8.

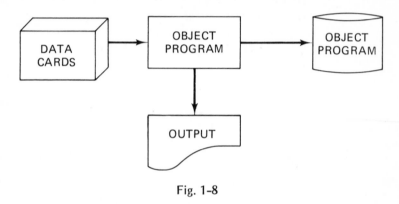

Fig. 1-8

PL/C Compiler

The PL/C compiler was developed primarily for educational institutes by Cornell University. It is particularly noted for fast compile times and exceptionally good diagnostics. A compile in PL/C consists of the compiler being brought into main storage from a direct access device. All compiling and executing of the program is done in main storage without the use of the disk. This is one of the principal reasons for the speed of PL/C (see Fig. 1-9). Because of the different operating characteristics of PL/C, the job control setup is different than for other PL/I compilers. If you are using PL/C, it is recommended that you contact your computer center for Job Control instructions.

Data Cards

Often information is supplied on cards to be read by the program. These data cards follow the source program in the card reader. They will not be read until the object program has been loaded into core and execution begins.

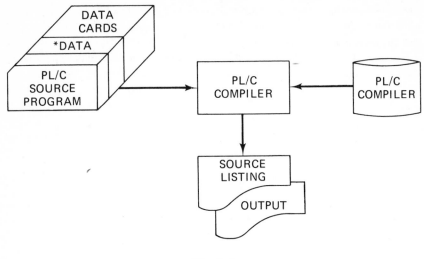

Fig. 1–9

At this time a GET or READ statement in the PL/I program will cause the information in the data card to be transferred to the program. Subsequent references to the GET or READ statement will cause additional data to be read from the following data cards. Data could also be read from other devices such as magnetic disks or tapes.

Job Control Language

Most modern computer systems contain a supervisor or control program which constantly monitors the compilation and execution of all other programs in the system. This control program requires some direction from the programmer in order for it to do its required tasks. This direction is given in the form of a Job Control Language. Job control varies a great deal from one system to another so it is advisable to inquire into the requirements of the system you may be using.

Some commonly used Job Control Languages on System/370 are TOS (Tape Operating System), DOS (Disk Operating System), and OS (Operating System). See Appendix H for some sample JCL setups.

These cards will cause the PL/I source program to be read by the PL/I compiler and translated into machine language. This machine language (object) program is then loaded into main storage and executed.

Initially a program may require several compiles and executions before it is ready for use. This process is called debugging or testing. The first bugs (errors) that must be eliminated are those indicated as diagnostics by the compiler. Unfortunately the compiler cannot detect all errors and has particular problems detecting logical errors. It is therefore important to provide adequate test data when debugging a program to ensure its accuracy and dependability. This test data will aid greatly in detecting logical errors in the program.

2

PL/I Fundamentals

In Chapter 1 we discussed the general format used for coding PL/I source programs and the writing of statements and statement labels. In coding, the source program characters are selected from one of two possible character sets. The set you choose will depend upon the computer available for compiling your programs.

60-Character Set

The 60-character set is composed of 60 digits, alphabetic, and special characters. The set includes the ten digits 0 through 9. The 26 alphabetic characters A through Z are preceded by the dollar sign $, the number sign #, and the "at" or "each" sign @. These are considered to be alphabetic characters, thus making a total of 29 alphabetic characters. Finally there are 21 special characters.

Figure 2-1 shows the 60-character set in its entirety, accompanied by equivalent punched card codes (Hollerith). It is important to note the sequence of these characters: special characters, alphabetic characters, and finally numeric digits. This is known as the *collating sequence.* This aspect becomes very important when we discuss comparison of data in Chapter 6.

CHARACTER	CARD CODE	CHARACTER	CARD CODE
blank	no punches	G	12-7
•	12-8-3	H	12-8
<	12-8-4	I	12-9
(	12-8-5	J	11-1
+	12-8-6	K	11-2
|	12-8-7	L	11-3
&	12	M	11-4
$	11-8-3	N	11-5
*	11-8-4	Ø	11-6
)	11-8-5	P	11-7
;	11-8-6	Q	11-8
¬	11-8-7	R	11-9
-	11	S	0-2
/	0-1	T	0-3
,	0-8-3	U	0-4
%	0-8-4	V	0-5
_	0-8-5	W	0-6
>	0-8-6	X	0-7
?	0-8-7	Y	0-8
:	8-2	Z	0-9
#	8-3	0	0
@	8-4	1	1
'	8-5	2	2
=	8-6	3	3
A	12-1	4	4
B	12-2	5	5
C	12-3	6	6
D	12-4	7	7
E	12-5	8	8
F	12-6	9	9

Fig. 2-1 *60-Character Set*

For special operations we can combine two of these symbols to give a special meaning. This is done with comment cards (discussed in Chapter 1) using /* and */ to indicate the beginning and end of a comment. Figure 2-2 shows the *composite* symbols.

COMPOSITE SYMBOLS	CARD PUNCH
<=	12–8–4, 8–6
‖	12–8–7, 12–8–7
**	11–8–4, 11–8–4
¬<	11–8–7, 12–8–4
¬>	11–8–7, 0–8–6
¬=	11–8–7, 8–6
>=	0–8–6, 8–6
/*	0–1, 11–8–4
*/	11–8–4, 0–1

Fig. 2-2 *60-Character Set Composite Symbols*

48-Character Set (PL/I only)

The 48 character set shown in Fig. 2-3 uses 48 of the characters from the 60 character set. The characters missing from the 60 character set are replaced by composite symbols as shown in Fig. 2-4. Only four characters are not given equivalent symbols. These are the "at" sign, the number sign, the break character (underscore) and the question mark. This does not create any serious difficulty since these characters are usually not essential to programming.

CHARACTER	CARD CODE	CHARACTER	CARD CODE
blank	no punches	M	11–4
.	12–8–3	N	11–5
(	12–8–5	Ø	11–6
+	12–8–6	P	11–7
$	11–8–3	Q	11–8
*	11–8–4	R	11–9
)	11–8–5	S	0–2
–	11	T	0–3
/	0–1	U	0–4
,	0–8–3	V	0–5
'	8–5	W	0–6

Fig. 2-3 *48-Character Set (PL/I only)*

CHARACTER	CARD CODE	CHARACTER	CARD CODE
=	8-6	X	0-7
A	12-1	Y	0-8
B	12-2	Z	0-9
C	12-3	0	0
D	12-4	1	1
E	12-5	2	2
F	12-6	3	3
G	12-7	4	4
H	12-8	5	5
I	12-9	6	6
J	11-1	7	7
K	11-2	8	8
L	11-3	9	9

Fig. 2-3   *48-Character Set (PL/I only)* (continued)

60-CHARACTER SET EQUIVALENT	COMPOSITE SYMBOL	CARD CODE		
:	••	12-8-3,	12-8-3	
<=	LE	11-3,	12-5	
||	CAT	12-3,	12-1,	0-3
**	**	11-8-4,	11-8-4	
¬<	NL	11-5,	11-3	
¬>	NG	11-5,	12-1	
¬=	NE	11-5,	12-5	
;	,.	0-8-3,	12-8-3	
&	AND	12-1,	11-5,	12-4
>=	GE	12-7,	12-5	
>	GT	12-7,	0-3	
<	LT	11-3,	0-3	
¬	NØT	11-5,	11-6,	0-3
|	ØR	11-6,	11-9	
/*	/*	0-1,	11-8-4	
*/	*/	11-8-4,	0-1	
%	//	0-1,	0-1	
=	EQ	8-6		

Fig. 2-4   *48-Character Set Composite Symbols*

Data Types

Data refers to information or arithmetic values used in a PL/I program. This data is accessed by using either a variable name or a constant. The statement

---

VØLUME = 3.1416*RADIUS* *2*HEIGHT;

---

could be used to compute the volume of a cylinder. In this statement the values 3.1416 and 2 are called *constants* (i.e., their values never change). RADIUS and HEIGHT are *variables* which can take on different values. VØLUME is also a variable since its value depends upon the value of RADIUS and HEIGHT.

Values are originally read as input data and assigned to variable names in the program. This original data can be in a number of different forms. We are now going to examine six of these source data forms.

1. Decimal Fixed-point Data

Decimal fixed-point data consists of one or more decimal digits including an optional decimal point. If there is no decimal point the number is assumed to be an integer. A sign may precede the data to indicate positive or negative values.

The maximum number of decimal digits allowed is 15. The decimal point or sign is not considered as one of these digits.

Some examples of valid decimal fixed-point data are:

$$3.1416$$
$$25$$
$$350.$$
$$.750$$
$$.0001$$
$$06$$
$$+3.05$$
$$-0.05$$

2. Binary Fixed-point Data

Binary fixed-point data consists of one or more binary digits followed immediately by the letter B. The numbers 0 and 1 are the only valid binary digits.

The maximum number of binary digits permitted is 31. Fractional parts and binary points are not permitted in a binary number. The binary point is always assumed to follow the rightmost digit. A sign may be used to indicate positive or negative values.

Some examples of valid binary fixed-point data are:

101B
1111B
1B
0B
+10B
-11011B

In PL/I, binary fixed data are generally used when the ultimate in efficiency is required in computations. If a very long series of calculations are to be done in a program they will be done in less time if binary fixed data are used as opposed to decimal fixed data.

3. Decimal Floating-point Data

Occasionally we encounter values which are of a greater magnitude than can be represented in the decimal fixed-point form or are rather awkward to express as fixed-point numbers.

For example the distance to the nearest star is 25,000,000,000,000 miles. Such numbers are so cumbersome that an improved method of representing them is desirable.

Large numbers can be represented more easily using powers of 10.

$$10^1 = 10$$
$$10^2 = 100$$
$$10^3 = 1000$$
$$10^4 = 10000$$
$$10^5 = 100000$$
$$10^6 = 1000000$$
$$10^{15} = 1000000000000000$$

This is fine for multiples of 10 but the distance to the nearest star does not quite fit this pattern. It could, however, be written as:

$$25 \times 10^{12}$$

which means of course:

$$25 \times 1,000,000,000,000 = 25,000,000,000,000$$

It could also be written as:

$$250 \times 10^{11}$$

or

$$2.5 \times 10^{13}$$

All of these forms represent the same value.

In PL/I the decimal part of the data cannot exceed 16 digits. The exponent is limited to two digits within a range of approximately 10^{-78} to 10^{75}. In PL/I the value 25×10^{12} is represented as

$$25E12$$

The letter E indicates the decimal exponent is to follow. The decimal field and the exponent may each contain plus or minus signs.

Some examples of valid decimal floating-point data and their equivalent values are:

37E6	37,000,000
-732E2	-73,200
5E-3	.005
-5E-3	-.005
5.732E-3	.005732
+.05E+2	5

4. Binary Floating-point Data

The binary floating-point data are similar to decimal floating-point except it consists of a binary number followed by a decimal integer. The maximum number of binary digits permitted is 53 and the exponent may be three digits within a range of from 2^{-260} to 2^{252}.

Thus the binary value $1011000000 = 1011 \times 2^6$ is represented by 1011E6B.

The character B identifies this as being a binary value. Plus and minus signs may precede the binary field and the exponent.

Some examples of valid binary floating-point data and their equivalent values are:

101E5B	10100000
1.01E10B	10100000000
.11011E-1B	.011011
-1.1E2B	-110
-101E-5B	-.00101
+1100E+5B	110000000

5. Character String Data

Character string data consists of one or more digits, letters, special characters, or blanks. Any character which is valid for a given computer configuration may be used.

The maximum length permitted for a character string is 255 characters.

When character strings appear in data cards they may appear as shown in the following examples:

> INVENTØRY
> TAX RATE
> DATA PROCESSING
> 195 EAST 22ND STREET
> #25
> AB73*_

When character strings are used in the program they must always be enclosed in apostrophes as shown:

> 'PAYRØLL'
> 'CØMPUTER PRØGRAMMING'
> '2755 YØNGE STREET'
> '25_75_1'
> 'XYZ*7'

If the character string is to contain an apostrophe within it, two apostrophes must be used. For example the character string

> EMPLØYEE'S BENEFITS

would be written in a program as

> 'EMPLØYEE''S BENEFITS'

The double apostrophe requires two card columns but counts as only one character and occupies only one storage position.

6. Bit String Data

Bit string data consists of one or more binary digits. A bit string can consist of a maximum of 64 bits. Since this is also string data it is written as we wrote character string data except it is followed by the letter B.

Some examples of bit string data in a program are as follows:

> '0'B
> '1'B

'010011'B
'100001100'B

Identifiers

A PL/I program manipulates the data described under "Data Types" to produce reports, updated files, calculated values, etc. This process requires the ability to refer to the data and perform arithmetic, comparison, and assignment operations on it. This is accomplished through the use of *identifiers*.

Each data item is given a unique identifier so that it may be referred to independent of all other data items. An identifier, like a statement label, is a character string of up to 31 characters. In PL/C an identifier may not be a keyword. See Appendix G.

For example, data cards may be read which contain the following information:

	CARD COLUMNS	TYPE OF DATA
(1)	1–8	Payroll Number
(2)	9–30	Employee Name
(3)	31–33	Hours Worked
(4)	34–37	Hourly Rate
(5)	38–40	Tax Rate

This data card might be organized as shown in Fig. 2–5. The names at the bottom could be used as identifiers in the program to refer to these fields.

In the program these fields are referred to by identifiers. We might choose the following names:

(1) PAYRØLL
(2) NAME
(3) HØURS
(4) RATE
(5) TAX

Or if we wished we could choose a different set of names such as:

(1) PAYRØLL_NUMBER
(2) EMP_NAME
(3) HRS_WØRKED
(4) HØURLY_RATE
(5) TAX_RATE

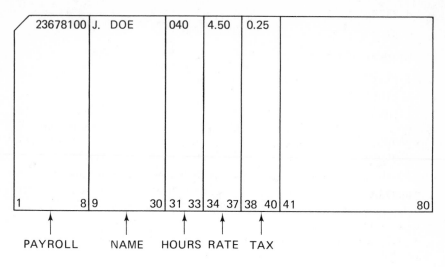

Fig. 2-5

At this stage, the name we choose is not too significant. However, once a name is chosen to represent a given data item, we must always use that name in that program.

Once identifiers have been established, we may use them to produce required information. In this case we might wish to compute GRØSS_SALARY. This could be done as follows:

GRØSS_SALARY = HRS_WØRKED∗HØURLY_RATE;

This is an arithmetic statement which causes HRS_WØRKED to be multiplied by HØURLY_RATE and the result assigned to the data item called GRØSS_SALARY. Arithmetic statements will be described in detail in Chapter 4.

In the next chapter we will see how the identifier is related to the actual data item by using a declare statement.

Exercises

1. Which of the following are valid decimal fixed-point data?

    a. −1.010   f. 29

    b. 1101B   g. 1/2

    c. 45E10   h. .000

d. 23701567 .3790245   i. 2^3

e. 37.5+   j. 0.333333333333333

2. Which of the following are invalid binary fixed-point data?

   a. +111B   d. 2B

   b. 11011111011   e. 11.01B

   c. 1010.1E101

3. Identify the following values as being decimal fixed, binary fixed, decimal float, or binary float.

   a. −1B   f. 1.001

   b. 273E−8   g. 10

   c. 1.1E7B   h. −11.11E1

   d. −1   i. 1E175B

   e. 10B   j. +3.0070

4. Show how the following data may be represented as character strings.

   a. WANDA DRAYTØN   d. JACK'S

   b. 2800 EAST 33RD STREET   e. "QUØTES"

   c. 47359

5. Represent the following as bit strings.

   a. 1100

   b. 00

   c. 111111

   d. 2

6. Which of the following are valid identifiers?

   a. QUANTITY   d. #10

   b. TEN   e. $_AND_CENTS

   c. 10

7. Choose appropriate identifiers for the fields in the following data card.

1-5	Product Number
6-15	Description
16-19	Storage Location
20-24	In Stock Quantity
25-29	Weighted Average Cost
30-34	Reorder Quantity
35-39	On Order Quantity

3

Declarations

In Chapter 2 the various data types such as decimal fixed-point and character string data were examined. It was discovered that each data type had its own method of representing data in a constant form. In PL/I it is necessary, in most cases, to refer to these data items by use of symbolic names called identifiers. These identifiers are sometimes called *variable names.*

The Declare statement is used to associate a variable name with the data itself. The Declare also specifies the type of data expected on the input media and reserves main storage space for this data. When writing a DECLARE, the statement consists of an identifier followed by a series of attributes. These attributes specify the form the data is to take. This could be DECIMAL or BINARY, FIXED, or FLØAT. Figure 3-1 shows the general format for a declare statement.

---

1 2

      DECLARE *identifier base scale (precision),*
                 identifier base scale (precision);

Fig. 3-1

DECLARE   Is the keyword which begins each Declare statement. DECLARE may be abbreviated to DCL (see Appendix A).

identifier   Is a variable name consisting of a string of
                                          up to 31 alphanumeric characters and break
                                          characters. The initial character of the *iden-
                                          tifier* must be alphabetic.

base   The base attribute specifies whether the vari-
                                          able is to be binary or decimal. The key-
                                          words BINARY or DECIMAL can be used as
                                          base attributes.

scale   The scale attribute specifies whether the vari-
                                          able is to be fixed or float. The keywords
                                          FIXED or FLØAT can be used as scale attri-
                                          butes.

(precision)   The precision attribute can be written in the
                                          form (l,d) for DECIMAL FIXED or (l) for
                                          other data types.

                                          (l,d) In this format the letter l specifies the
                                                   length of the data item. It does not in-
                                                   clude the decimal point if one exists.
                                                   The character d specifies the number
                                                   of digits to the right of the decimal
                                                   point. If d is zero, it may be omitted.

                                          (l)   This format is used to specify the
                                                   length for decimal float, binary fixed,
                                                   and float data items.

Decimal Fixed

Suppose a program reads student record data containing variables such as student number, semester, number of courses, cost per course, student fees, and
total tuition. In order to declare variables for this information, the data must be
examined to determine the type of attributes to use in the declare. The data
might look like this:

DATA NAMES	DATA VALUES
Student number	700236101
Semester	3
Number of courses	5
Cost per course	60.00
Student fees	35.00
Total tuition	335.00

These numbers are all DECIMAL FIXED with varying precisions depending upon the nature of the data. Now proceed to declare each item. Student number consists of 9 decimal digits with no decimal point. The student number can be declared as:

DECLARE STUDENT_NUMBER DECIMAL FIXED (9);

This reserves storage for a variable called STUDENT_NUMBER and indicates that it is a DECIMAL FIXED number consisting of nine digits. The precision attribute can also be written as:

(9,0)

Likewise, proceed to declare Semester and Number of Courses as follows:

DECLARE SEMESTER DECIMAL FIXED (1);

DECLARE NUM_CØURSES DECIMAL FIXED (1);

The final three items contain a decimal point and a fractional part. Remember that in determining the number of digits, the decimal point is not included. Thus these variables are declared as follows:

DECLARE CØST_PER_CØURSE DECIMAL FIXED (4,2);

DECLARE STUDENT_FEES DECIMAL FIXED (4,2);

DECLARE TØTAL_TUITIØN DECIMAL FIXED (5,2);

As shown in the general format in Fig. 3-1, several variables may be grouped together in one declare statement. The length may also be reduced by the use of abbreviations.

```
DCL   S_NUM        DEC FIXED (9),
      SEM          DEC FIXED (1),
      N_CØURSES    DEC FIXED (1),
      CØST         DEC FIXED (4,2),
      FEES         DEC FIXED (4,2),
      TUITIØN      DEC FIXED (5,2);
```

The end of each variable declared is followed by a comma. A semicolon terminates the final declaration.

Binary Fixed

In Chapter 2 some examples of valid binary fixed-point data were examined. These values are shown here with associated data names.

DATA NAMES	DATA VALUES
FLDA	101B
FLDB	1111B
FLDC	1B
FLDD	0B
FLDE	+10B
FLDF	-11011B

These data items can be declared as follows:

```
DCL        FLDA BINARY FIXED (3),
           FLDB BINARY FIXED (4),
           FLDC BINARY FIXED (1),
           FLDD BINARY FIXED (1),
           FLDE BINARY FIXED (2),
           FLDF BINARY FIXED (5);
```

Decimal Float

A similar approach to the above is used when declaring decimal float numbers. In this case count the number of digits to the left of the E in the floating-point number when evaluating the precision attribute.

DATA NAMES	DATA VALUES
FLD_1	37E6
FLD_2	-732E2
FLD_3	5E-3
FLD_4	-5E-3
FLD_5	5.732E-2
FLD_6	+.05E+2

These data items are declared as follows:

```
DCL    FLD_1 DEC FLØAT (2),
       FLD_2 DEC FLØAT (3),
       FLD_3 DEC FLØAT (1),
       FLD_4 DEC FLØAT (1),
       FLD_5 DEC FLØAT (4),
       FLD_6 DEC FLØAT (2);
```

Notice particularly the precision for FLD_5. The digits on both sides of the decimal point must be considered when determining the length.

Binary Float

The declaration of binary float data is similar to decimal float except of course for the base attribute. Notice again that only the digits in the mantissa are counted when determining the precision.

DATA NAMES	DATA VALUES
VALUEA	101E5B
VALUEB	1.01E10B
VALUEC	.11011E–1B
VALUED	–1.1E2B
VALUEE	–101E–5B
VALUEF	+1100E+5B

These data items are declared as follows:

```
DCL    VALUEA BINARY FLØAT (3),
       VALUEB BINARY FLØAT (3),
       VALUEC BINARY FLØAT (5),
       VALUED BINARY FLØAT (2),
       VALUEE BINARY FLØAT (3),
       VALUEF BINARY FLØAT (4);
```

The examples used have shown declares with only one type of variable. There is no reason why these cannot be mixed if the occasion demands.

```
DCL    S_NUM DEC FIXED (9),
       FLDA BINARY FIXED (3),
       FLD_I DEC FLØAT (2),
       VALUEA BINARY FLØAT (3);
```

This approach may be taken when four different types of variables are needed in the same program.

It is important in the case of arithmetic variables to ensure that the precision attribute chosen adequately handles all possible data. For example, the variable declared as

DCL FEES DEC FIXED (4,2);

would permit a maximum value of 99.99. If the fee in one case happened to be 105.00 this would be stored in the variable FEES as 05.00 because there is no room for the hundreds position. Conversely, if the fee was 5.00 it would be stored as 05.00.

The high order zero is added to fill the variable so that it contains four numeric digits.

Factoring

For ease of programming, identifiers which use the same base, scale, and precision attributes may be grouped together. In the example of the binary floating-point declares, VALUEA, VALUEB, and VALUEE all use the same attributes. They could be declared as:

DCL (VALUEA, VALUEB, VALUEE) BINARY FLØAT(3);

The identifiers are grouped together within parentheses and separated by commas. They are then followed by the base, scale, and precision attributes. This involves writing the attributes only once as opposed to the original three times.

String Data

Character Strings

In business data processing applications, it is unusual to have data files which do not contain some alphanumeric data. Thus, it is common to deal with variables such as name, address, city, and descriptions of many types. Character string variables must be declared to permit the computer to manipulate the information in PL/I. The general format is given in Fig. 3-2.

1	2

DECLARE *identifier* CHARACTER (*length*);

Fig. 3-2

DECLARE	Keyword.
identifier	Any legal variable name.
CHARACTER	Keyword which specifies a character string variable. CHARACTER may be abbreviated to CHAR (see Appendix A).
(*length*)	Length in PL/C is a decimal integer containing a value from 1 to 256 enclosed in parentheses. In the PL/1 optimizer length may be a maximum of 32,767.
	Semicolon terminates the declare. As stated previously, several variables may be declared in a single declare statement by separating them with commas.

The declare is demonstrated using the following examples.

DATA NAMES	DATA VALUES
FILE	'PAYRØLL'
ØCCUPATION	'CØMPUTER PRØGRAMMER'
ADDRESS	'2755 YØNGE STREET'
DATE	'10_07_71'
HDG	'EMPLØYEE''S BENEFITS'

Using the CHARACTER attribute, these variables would be declared as follows:

DCL	FILE	CHARACTER (7),
	ØCCUPATIØN	CHARACTER (19),
	ADDRESS	CHARACTER (17),
	DATE	CHARACTER (8),
	HDG	CHARACTER (19);

Notice that in the variable named HDG the length is 19, not 20. Recall that the paired apostrophes only count as one unit, not two. If the length had been miscalculated, the data value would not necessarily be stored as required.

Suppose ØCCUPATION had been declared as CHARACTER (18). The resultant data value when assigned to ØCCUPATION would be CØMPUTER PRØGRAMME, not CØMPUTER PRØGRAMMER. The low-order character was truncated since there is no room for it. If ØCCUPATIØN had been declared as CHARACTER(20), CØMPUTER PRØGRAMMERb would result.

In this case, a blank is added to the low order position to make up the difference in length. Since a blank does not actually print on output it is possible that it would not be evident that this condition had occurred.

Bit Strings

Recall from Chapter 2 that a bit string consists of a string of zeros and ones. The format and rules for declaring a bit string are very similar to the character string. The general format is shown in Fig. 3-3.

---

1 | 2

DECLARE *identifier* BIT (*length*);

Fig. 3-3

DECLARE	Keyword
identifier	Any legal variable name.
BIT	Keyword which specifies a bit string.
(*length*)	Length in PL/C is a decimal integer with a value of 1 to 256 contained within parentheses. The maximum is 32,767 in the PL/I optimizer.
;	Semicolon terminates the declare.

Using the bit string values repeated here from Chapter 2 gives the following:

DATA NAMES	DATA VALUES
SWA	'0'B
SWB	'1'B
STRNG	'010011'B
NINE	'100001100'B

```
DCL    (SWA,SWB) BIT (1),
       STRNG BIT (6),
       NINE BIT (9);
```

Since SWA and SWB each need to contain only one bit their identifiers may be grouped together in the declare statement.

As with character strings, it is important that the length attribute is correctly determined. If the length is shorter than the data value, truncation will occur on the right-most (low-order) bit(s).

Using the bit string STRNG as an example, observe that if the declare had been

```
DCL STRNG BIT(5);
```

and if the data value '010011'B is assigned to the variable the result would be 01001 with the low-order 1 being truncated.

In the case of the length being too long, low order zeros are added to the bit string value.

Therefore if the declare had been

```
DCL STRNG BIT(8);
```

and '010011'B is assigned to STRNG, the result will be 01001100 which includes two low-order zeroes.

Notice that for bit strings the data is always left-adjusted in the field and low-order zeroes are added if necessary. Conversely binary data is right-adjusted with high order zeroes added if necessary.

Defaults

When variables are defined in a declare statement this is known as explicit declaration. This term is used since the attributes which represent the variable explicitly state how that variable is to exist in the program. In PL/I a default system exists which permits the programmer to use variable names without declaring them first. When a variable which has not been declared is used, the PL/I compiler assumes certain default attributes. This process is known as implicit declaration.

The defaults taken when implicit declaration occurs are based on a simple rule. If the first character of the variable name begins with the letters I, J, K, L, M, or N, the variable defaults to

BINARY FIXED (15);

When the variable name begins with characters other than I-N, including alphabetic substitute characters $, #, and @, the default is

DECIMAL FLØAT (6);

If the variable names in Fig. 3-4 were used in a program without being previously declared, the indicated attributes would be assumed by the compiler.

VARIABLE NAME	DEFAULT
NUM	BINARY FIXED (15)
I	BINARY FIXED (15)
TØTAL	DECIMAL FLØAT (6)
#12	DECIMAL FLØAT (6)

Fig. 3-4 *Implicit Declaration*

The default system also applies to variables which are explicitly declared but without all the necessary attributes. Fig. 3-5 shows the precision defaults when both base and scale are present.

BASE AND SCALE ATTRIBUTES (Explicitly Declared)	PRECISION ATTRIBUTE (Default)
DECIMAL FIXED	(5,0)
DECIMAL FLØAT	(6)
BINARY FIXED	(15)
BINARY FLØAT	(21)

Fig. 3-5 *Precision Defaults*

Figure 3-6 shows the defaults taken when the base or scale attributes are missing. Precision may or may not be present with base or scale default. When it is not present, it also defaults according to Fig. 3-5. If precision is present, it is important that its form corresponds with the defaulting base or scale attribute. That is, if DECIMAL were the explicitly declared attribute, the explicit precision could not be in the form (7,2). This precision is valid only for DECIMAL FIXED, but in this case the scale attribute would default to FLØAT.

BASE OR SCALE ATTRIBUTE (Explicitly Declared)	DEFAULT
DECIMAL	FLØAT
BINARY	FLØAT
FIXED	DECIMAL
FLØAT	DECIMAL

Fig. 3-6 *Base and Scale Defaults*

Figure 3-7 shows various combinations of declarations and the resulting defaults. This system of defaults can be an advantage to the programmer by reducing the number of declare statements written in a PL/I program. It is important that caution is exercised when permitting defaults since it is easy to get an unexpected default if the rules are not carefully followed. From a documentation point of view, it is sometimes considered better to declare all variables explicitly so that immediate reference can be made to their specific attributes.

EXPLICIT DECLARATION	RESULT INCLUDING THE DEFAULTS
DCL NUM1 FIXED,	DCL NUM1 FIXED DECIMAL (5,0),
NUM2 FLØAT,	NUM2 FLØAT DECIMAL (6),
NUM3 DECIMAL,	NUM3 DECIMAL FLØAT (6),
NUM4 BINARY,	NUM4 BINARY FLØAT (21),
VALA DECIMAL FIXED,	VALA DECIMAL FIXED (5,0),
VALB DECIMAL FLØAT,	VALB DECIMAL FLØAT (6),
VALC BINARY FIXED,	VALC BINARY FIXED (15),
VALD BINARY FLØAT,	VALD BINARY FLØAT (21),
IN FIXED (5,3),	IN FIXED DECIMAL (5,3),
ØUT DECIMAL (16);	ØUT DECIMAL FLØAT (16);

Fig. 3-7

Initial Attribute

In most programs, there are certain variables which must begin with a predefined value. A common example of this is a variable which is used to accumulate a total to be printed at the end of the program. A total field must always start with a zero value, otherwise a computer interrupt may occur. An interrupt occurs when the computer is asked to execute a statement, but for various reasons cannot do so. For instance, an attempt to add two pieces of non-numeric data would cause an interrupt.

Another case where initial values may be used is in a program which is written to solve a very specific problem such as calculating the volume of a cube. In this situation, begin with initial values for length, width and depth and then use the variable names in the program to perform the calculation.

Figure 3-8 shows the general format of the initial attribute for arithmetic values.

---

1 | 2

DCL identifier base scale (precision) INITIAL (value);

Fig. 3-8

INITIAL	Keyword which identifies the presence of an initial value. This keyword always follows the declaration of some arithmetic variable. The abbreviation INIT is permitted.
(value)	*Value* is some arithmetic value contained in parenthesis. It must correspond with the format specified by the base, scale and precision attributes.

The following examples demonstrate the use of the INITIAL attribute.

```
DCL    TØTALA DECIMAL FIXED (7,2) INITIAL (00000.00),
       TØTALB DECIMAL FIXED (7,2) INITIAL (0),
       LENGTH BINARY FIXED (5) INITIAL (11011B),
       WIDTH BINARY FIXED (4) INITIAL (111B),
       DEPTH BINARY FIXED (4) INITIAL (1011B);
```

Notice that the resulting initial value for TØTALA and TØTALB will be identical. WIDTH will include a high order zero since the value specified is shorter than the declared field. The plus or minus sign may precede the initial value as follows:

```
DCL VALUE DEC FIXED (3,1) INIT (-27.8);
```

The initial attribute for character and bit strings is slightly different than for arithmetic values. This general format is shown in Fig. 3–9.

1│2

DCL *identifier* CHARACTER *or* BIT (*length*) INITIAL ('*data*');

Fig. 3–9

INITIAL	Keyword
('*data*')	*Data* consists of a valid character string of up to **256** characters in length. If *data* is to be a bit string the letter B must follow the string after the closing quotation ('*data*'B).

Initial values for character string variables are commonly used in business applications for page headings on reports.

DCL   HEADA CHARACTER (14) INITIAL ('PAYRØLL REPØRT'),
        ADR CHAR(20) INIT ('STREET CITY PRØVINCE'),
        STNGA BIT (4) INIT ('1010'B),
        STNGB BIT (6) INIT ('1101'B);

The length attribute should always provide adequate space for the initial data including the imbedded blanks. STNGB has a length attribute which is 2 bits longer than the initial value. The result here would be 110100.

Repetition Factor

A repetition factor may be used with the INITIAL attribute if the data is to be repeated. The declare

---

DCL PAR CHARACTER (12) INITIAL ((2)'X Y Z ');

would repeat the initial data twice giving

X Y Z X Y Z

Declaring

DCL ZERØES CHAR (10) INIT ((10) '0');

---

would give an initial value of

0000000000

The same approach applies to bit strings.

DCL ØNES BIT (8) INIT ((8) '1'B);

---

would give

'11111111'B

Sample Program

Figure 3-10 shows a program which utilizes some of the knowledge gained from this chapter. The program, taken from the communications field, computes the length of a long wire transmitting antenna based upon the frequency of the signal to be transmitted. The formula used is

$$\text{Length (feet)} = \frac{492(N - 0.05)}{\text{Frequency (MHZ)}}$$

where N is the number of half waves on the antenna.

```
ANT: PROC OPTIONS(MAIN);
DCL  CONSTANT FIXED(3) INIT(492),
     FREQUENCY FIXED(5,3),
     LENGTH FIXED(4,1);
DCL L CHAR(38) INIT('THE LENGTH OF A LONG WIRE ANTENNA FOR'),
    M CHAR(13) INIT('MEGAHERTZ IS'),
    F CHAR(5) INIT('FEET');
GET LIST (FREQUENCY,N);
LENGTH = (CONSTANT*(N-0.05))/FREQUENCY;
PUT LIST(L,FREQUENCY,M,LENGTH,F);
END ANT;
```

Fig. 3-10

In this program, a number of uses for declares are illustrated. The CØN-STANT value 492 is declared with an initial value. This is a matter of preference, as is shown by the usage of the constant 0.05. This value is not declared but is used directly in the arithmetic statement as a value (arithmetic statements are discussed in Chapter 4).

The values of FREQUENCY and LENGTH are yet unknown but if we know their approximate size, storage space may be reserved by a declare. The variable N is not declared but is used by the program. It will therefore default to BINARY FIXED(15).

The variables L,M, and F are not apparent from the formula given. However this approach is taken in most programs to make the resultant answers printed by the program more readable. Thus L, M, and F are declared with character string constants which will be used when printing the output.

Following the declares are a series of statements which constitute the program itself. The GET LIST is a statement which reads values for FREQUENCY and N from a data card (see Chapter 5).

The next statement is an arithmetic statement which computes the value of LENGTH using the values presently stored for CØNSTANT, N and FREQUENCY.

Finally the PUT LIST is used to print the result of the computation. If the data had been

FREQUENCY	N
12.000	2

the resulting printout would be

THE LENGTH OF A LONG WIRE ANTENNA FOR 14.210 MEGAHERTZ IS 32.0 FEET

Exercises

1. Write appropriate Declare statements for the following data.

   a. 378.6790   f. 0001B

   b. 0   g. 11.11E5

   c. 12.5E+10   h. .00789

   d. -00101B   i. 11.11E5B

   e. 295.   j. 1

2. What would the resultant data look like if the values under column A were assigned to the variables declared under column B?

A	B
a. 4.78	DCL A DECIMAL FIXED (5,2);
b. 3748.6	DCL B DECIMAL FIXED (5,2);

    c. 21.   DCL C DECIMAL FIXED (2);

    d. 101B   DCL D BINARY FIXED (4);

    e. 11011B   DCL E BINARY FIXED (4);

3. Write appropriate Declare statements for the following character and bit string data.

    a. 'SALES ANALYSIS'   d. '1100'B

    b. '28.570'   e. '1100'

    c. 'KEVIN''S'

4. List the resulting defaults for each of the following Declares.

    a. DCL JIM;   d. DCL TØTAL DECIMAL;

    b. DCL A;   e. DCL AMT (20);

    c. DCL CAT DECIMAL FIXED;   f. DCL QTY FLØAT (4);

5. Write Declares for the following data specifying the indicated values with an INITIAL attribute.

    a. 27.0   d. 110011001100 Binary

    b. -.005   e. GRØSS SALARY

    c. 110011001100 Bit String

Expressions

4

Thus far the PL/I program statements discussed may be considered as compiler-directing. The declare statements have directed the compiler to reserve storage which will be used at object program execution time. These declares do not normally cause any action to occur during program execution, only prior to execution.

The main body of the program contains statements which are used at the time of execution. These are the statements which represent the logic of the program. They specify how the computer is to go about solving the problem. A statement of this type is known as an expression.

An expression can appear in many forms but generally is used to represent some value. This value can be a single constant, a variable or an arithmetic statement. The general format of an expression is shown in Fig. 4-1.

1	2
	element-variable = element-expression;

Fig. 4-1 *Expressions*

element-variable	Any variable name. May have been specified in a declare statement or may be established based on the default rules.

39

=   Equal sign always separates the element-vari-
                                 able from the element-expression. The equal
                                 sign means "assign to." The value of the ele-
                                 ment-expression is assigned to the element-
                                 variable.

element-expression   Any valid expression which when evaluated
                                 represents a single value.

;   Semicolon terminates the statement.

Assignment of Data

A common use for an expression is to assign a value to some variable name.
This has already been done using an initial attribute in a declare statement. However, during the execution of a program, we may wish to change these initial
values. At this time a change may only be made with an assignment statement
(*expression*). Figure 4-2 shows some examples of valid assignments.

```
NUMBER      = 125;
QTY         = 60;
VALUE       = 73.65;
NAME        = 'JØHN DØE';
BITS        = '101101'B;
BINARY_ØNE = 1B;
```

Fig. 4-2 *Valid Assignments*

In this example the value on the right of the equal sign is assigned to the
variable named on the left of the equal sign. Thus, after the first statement is
executed, NUMBER will have the value of 125 regardless of what it had previously.

Of course it was assumed that the element-variables were all declared correctly. If NAME were not declared as CHARACTER we would get a diagnostic
to tell us that an invalid assignment was attempted.

Figure 4-3 shows a series of declares with some valid and invalid assignments.

```
DCL   ADDRESS CHAR (20),
      AMØUNTA FIXED (5,2),
      AMØUNTB FIXED (5,2),
      SWITCH BIT (1),
      TØTAL BINARY (6);
```

ADDRESS	= '175 EASTERN BLVD';	Valid
AMØUNTA	= 125.75;	Valid
AMØUNTA	= 2.36;	Valid
AMØUNTB	= '125.75';	Invalid
SWITCH	= '1'B;	Valid
SWITCH	= '1';	Invalid
SWITCH	= 1B;	Invalid
TØTAL	= 11011B;	Valid
TØTAL	= 27;	Valid

Fig. 4-3

In the case of ADDRESS, only 16 characters are being assigned to a 20-character field. Therefore the data is left-adjusted and low-order blanks inserted. The second assignment to AMØUNTA will result in a value of 002.36. AMØUNTB is an invalid assignment since the value is a character string. The final assignment may appear to be invalid since 27 is not a binary number. However, in this case, the computer can convert the decimal value 27 to its equivalent binary value. This may be less efficient than assigning the binary value directly but it relieves the programmer of the burden of making the conversion. See Appendix B for valid conversions.

PL/I is not limited to assigning constants to variable names. Variables can be assigned to other variable names. If AMØUNTA contains a certain value and we wish AMØUNTB to contain the same value we write AMØUNTA to the right of the equal sign.

$$AMØUNTB = AMØUNTA;$$

This statement takes whatever value is presently in AMØUNTA and assigns it to AMØUNTB. Thus AMØUNTA and AMØUNTB will both contain the same value after this statement is executed.

BEFØRE EXECUTING	275.65	001.00
ASSIGNMENT STATEMENT	AMØUNTA	AMØUNTB
AFTER EXECUTING	275.65	275.65
ASSIGNMENT STATEMENT	AMØUNTA	AMØUNTB

Notice that AMØUNTA does not change in value. This is a very important aspect of expressions. The variable or expression on the right of the equal sign never changes in value. The variable on the left of the equal sign always changes and takes on the value of the variable or expression on the right-hand side.

There are times when data is assigned to variables which consist of different attributes than the source data. Examples of this are given in Fig. 4-4. This table assumes the use of B = A;

A		B	
Attributes	Value	Attributes	Value
FIXED(5,2)	207.53	FIXED(4,2)	07.53
		FIXED(5,1)	207.5
		FIXED(2,2)	.53
		FIXED(5)	00207.
BINARY FIXED(4)	1101	BINARY FIXED(2)	01
		BINARY FIXED(5)	01101
		FIXED(2)	13
CHAR(7)	'EXAMPLE'	CHAR(4)	'EXAM'
		CHAR(9)	'EXAMPLEƀƀ'

Fig. 4-4

In the case of numeric data, if B is shorter than A, truncation occurs on the left for the integer part. For the fractional part, truncation occurs on the right. If B is longer than A, additional zeros are inserted to make up the difference.

　　In the case of character strings, truncation occurs on the right when B is shorter. When B is longer, spaces are appended to the right of the data.

Arithmetic Operations

The next step in the use of expressions in PL/I deals with arithmetic statements. These are used for performing arithmetic calculations. There are five types of arithmetic operators:

+	addition
–	subtraction
*	multiplication
/	division
* *	exponentiation

　　In addition, the prefix + and the prefix – are available in PL/I. A discussion of their usage is found at the end of this chapter.

　　Suppose two values, VALUE and AMØUNT, are to be added together and the result placed in a variable called TØTAL. Figure 4–5 shows how this is done and the values of each field before and after the operation.

```
DCL     VALUE FIXED (4,1) INIT (215.0),
        AMØUNT FIXED (4,2) INIT (04.00),
        TØTAL FIXED (5,2) INIT (0);

        TØTAL = AMØUNT + VALUE;
```

BEFORE	215.0	04.00	000.00
AFTER	215.0	04.00	219.00
	VALUE	AMØUNT	TOTAL

Fig. 4-5

The decimal value in the location named AMØUNT is arithmetically added to the decimal value in the location named VALUE and the result of this addition is assigned to the location named TØTAL. AMØUNT and VALUE remain unaffected by this operation. This calculation looks similar to the algebraic statement

$$total = amount + value$$

or

$$t = a + v$$

An arithmetic statement should not be confused with the algebraic statement. The algebraic version means that t is equal to the total of a and v. That is, only those values of a and v whose total is equal to t are valid numbers for a and v. In PL/I, TØTAL may or may not have a value. The values in AMØUNT and VALUE are added together without regard to a possible value in TØTAL.

The result of this addition is placed in TØTAL thus destroying any previous value TØTAL may have had. The arithmetic plus sign used in this context is called an "infix +." Similarly, the other arithmetic operators are used as follows.

Subtraction

```
            VALUE   = 25.0;
            AMØUNT =  6.0;
            DIFF    = VALUE - AMØUNT;
```

BEFORE	25.0	6.0	ANY VALUE
AFTER	25.0	6.0	19.0

VALUE   AMØUNT   DIFF

If DIFF = AMØUNT – VALUE; was written, the result in DIFF after executing the expression would be –19.0. In this case the rules of algebra apply when considering the signs of the values.

Multiplication

VALUE   = 25.0;
AMØUNT = 2.5;
PRØDUCT = VALUE * AMØUNT

BEFORE	25.0	2.5	ANY VALUE
AFTER	25.0	2.5	62.5

VALUE   AMØUNT   PRØDUCT

Here VALUE and AMØUNT are multiplied together and the result placed in PRØDUCT. In the case of signs the rules of algebra apply. Therefore if a negative value is multiplied by a positive, the result will be negative. A negative times a negative yields a positive.

Division

VALUE   = 150.0;
AMØUNT = 4.0;
QUØTIENT = VALUE/AMØUNT;

BEFORE	150.0	4.0	ANY VALUE
AFTER	150.0	4.0	37.5

VALUE   AMØUNT   QUØTIENT

Of course QUØTIENT must be declared with a precision of at least (3,1). If precision had been (4,2) the result would be 37.50.

Exponentiation

VALUE   = 12.0;
AMØUNT = 2.0;
RESULT = VALUE * * AMØUNT;

BEFORE	12.0	2.0	ANY VALUE
AFTER	12.0	2.0	144.0

VALUE   AMØUNT   RESULT

Figure 4-6 shows additional examples of simple arithmetic statements and the result of their execution.

EXPRESSION	A	B	RESULT
RESULT = A+B;	-2	2	0
RESULT = A+B;	-2	-2	-4
RESULT = A-B;	-5	7	-12
RESULT = A-B;	-5	-7	2
RESULT = A*B;	-3	5	-15
RESULT = A*B;	-7	-12	84
RESULT = A/B;	-8	2	-4
RESULT = A/B;	-8	-2	4

Fig. 4-6

Hierarchy

It is sometimes necessary to combine two or more of the arithmetic operators into one statement. For instance, the algebraic expression a+b/c is to be written in a PL/I statement giving

RESULT = A+B/C;

If the values of A, B and C are 6, 4 and 2 respectively then what will be the solution in RESULT? The solution depends upon which part of the expression is evaluated first. That is if A+B is evaluated and then divided by C the answer will be 5. However, if B/C is evaluated first then added to A the solution will be 8.

Conflicts of this nature are resolved by a hierarchical structure of arithmetic operators which establishes a *priority* for these operations. The hierarchy is shown in Fig. 4-7.

parenthesis   highest priority
* *   *prefix* + *prefix* –
*   /
infix + *infix* –   lowest priority

Fig. 4-7 *Hierarchy of Operators*

It is evident from Fig. 4-7 that division has a higher priority than addition. Thus in the expression

$$RESULT = A+B/C;$$

the first computation is B/C, the result of which is added together with A and assigned to RESULT giving 8 as the solution.

When two operators of the same level of priority appear in a statement, evaluation proceeds from left to right. Thus in RESULT = X*Y/Z; the solution will be developed by evaluating X*Y and dividing this by Z.

Sometimes conflicts arise which can easily be resolved through the use of parenthesis. Given the algebraic expression $\dfrac{a + b}{c/d}$, write an equivalent PL/I expression. Written simply, the expression might be RESULT = A+B/C/D;. Following the rules of hierarchy means that the first operation will be B/C. Obviously this is not correct according to the original expression. What is desired is to evaluate A+B, then C/D, and finally divide the result of these two separate evaluations. Using parenthesis gives a valid solution RESULT = (A+B)/(C/D);.

Parentheses have the highest priority and since two sets of them appear in this statement they are evaluated from left to right giving the correct solution.

An exception to this rule is when an expression of the form A = B**N**2; occurs. In this case exponentiation proceeds from right to left and N is raised to the power of 2. B is then raised to the power of this result.

Parentheses may also be contained within parentheses to control priority. Take the expression

$$n = \left(\frac{k + 5}{j - n^2} \right)^3$$

In PL/I we would write

$$N = ((K + 5) / (J - N**2)) ** 3;$$

The first operation would be K + 5 which is the first set, from left to right, of innermost brackets. Next would be J-N∗ ∗2 with exponentiation taking priority over subtraction. Then the division of these results occurs controlled by the outer brackets. Without the outer set, exponentiation to the power of 3 would take priority over division. Therefore the extra parentheses are required.

Infix and Prefix

The hierarchy of operators in Fig. 4-7 shows two different types of + and – called prefix + and – and infix + and –. Thus far all of the addition and subtraction has been of the infix variety. The infix operator always appears between two variable names. Thus

$$X = A+B;$$
$$X = A-B;$$
$$X = A+B-C;$$

all use infix operators.

Prefix operators always precede a variable name. Thus X = -A; assigns the negative value of A to X. If A had been negative the effect would be to assign the positive value of A to X.

$$A = --A;$$

has the effect of no sign. That is, the negative signs cancel each other.

$$X = A* -B;$$

Here A is multiplied by the negative value of B. The minus is a prefix operator. Figure 4-7 shows that the prefix operator is at the highest level of priority. If this is applied to the statement

$$X = A*-B* *2;$$

the first operation will be evaluating –B then raising this to the power of 2 and finally multiplying this result by A. Since the prefix – and exponentiation are of the same priority, processing occurs from left to right.

Mathematical Functions

Certain common mathematical functions such as finding square root, sine, or cosine are built into the PL/I compiler to provide convenience of use. Some of these functions would be much too complicated for the programmer to write each time they are needed. They may be made available by specifying certain function names.

In this chapter a few of the more common functions are discussed. For other functions, refer to Chapter 11.

Sqrt

This function finds the square root of a given expression. The general format is

$$v = \text{SQRT}(e);$$

where *v*	represents the variable which is to receive the result of the square root function
SQRT	is the function name
(*e*)	*e* is the expression of which the square root is taken.

Several examples of the use of this function follow:

$$X = \text{SQRT}(36);$$

This statement finds the square root of 36 and assigns the result 6 to the variable X.

The statement

$$A = \text{SQRT}(X);$$

finds the square root of the present value of X and assigns the result to A.

The expression may require evaluation as follows

$$\text{TABLE}(1) = \text{SQRT}(2*(X*(Y + 7.8)));$$

Here the expression $2*(X*(Y + 7.8))$ is evaluated. The square root is then taken of the result of this evaluation. The result is then assigned to the Ith position of the array TABLE. See Chapter 7 for arrays.

Sin

This function takes the sine of a given expression which must be in radians. The general format is

$$v = \text{SIN}(e);$$

where *v*   represents the variable which is to receive
                                         the result of the operation.

SIN   is the function name

(*e*)   is the expression, in radians, of which the
                                         sine is to be found.

The use of SIN is similar to SQRT as may be seen in the following example.

$$X = SIN(Y)$$

The sine of Y is computed and the result is assigned to X.

Cos

This function takes the cosine of a given expression in radians. The general
format is the same as for SIN.

$$v = COS(e);$$

where *v*   is the variable receiving the result of the
                                         cosine function.

COS   is the function name

(*e*)   is the expression, in radians, of which the
                                         cosine is to be found.

An example of use might be

$$C = COS(2*Y);$$

which takes the cosine of $(2*Y)$ and assigns the result to the variable C.

Concatenation

Combining several character or bit strings into one variable is known as concate-
nation. The concatenation operator is the symbol | |, which requires two card
columns.

Given two character strings MØNTH and DAY these can be combined with
an absolute value representing year to give a composite date. This is demonstrated
in Fig. 4-8.

```
DCL   MØNTH CHAR (2) INIT ('06'),
      DAY   CHAR (2) INIT ('27'),
      YEAR  CHAR (6);

YEAR = DAY||MØNTH||'77';
```

Fig. 4-8 *Concatenation*

The result of this operation in YEAR will be the value '270677'. This same method applies to bit strings.

$$
\text{ØNES} = \text{'1111'B};
$$
$$
\text{ZERØES} = \text{'0000'B};
$$
$$
\text{HØLD} = \text{ØNES}||\text{ZERØES};
$$

The value in HØLD will be '11110000'B after executing these statements.

For some applications it might be desirable to have YEAR in the form of 27/06/77. This can also be accomplished with concatenation. In this case YEAR must be declared with at least 8 characters. The expression used for this operation is:

$$
\text{YEAR} = \text{DAY} || \text{'/'} || \text{MONTH} || \text{'/'} || \text{'77'};
$$

This causes the literal '/' to be concatenated with DAY and MONTH to give the composite result we are looking for.

Substr—Sub-String Built-in Function

The SUBSTR function can be used to extract from a character string variable a select portion of the data. Normally when a character string is used in an assignment the data begins at the leftmost character and moves for the entire length of the field. This function permits the programmer to begin at any character position and move as many characters as desired. The general format for SUBSTR is shown in Fig. 4-9.

Suppose we have a variable declared

DCL NAME CHAR(9);

containing the data

NAME | A | J | S | I | M | P | S | O | N |

The first two characters are the initials and the rest the surname. We want to store these in the variables

DCL INITIALS   CHAR(2),
SURNAME CHAR(7);

To store the initials we write

INITIALS = SUBSTR(NAME,1,2);

This moves two characters of data beginning at the first byte of NAME. These two characters are the letters AJ, the initials. To move the surname SIMPSON write

SURNAME = SUBSTR(NAME,3,7);

Now suppose we want to store AJ as

| A | . | J | . |

including the periods to indicate an abbreviation. This requires A and J to be moved separately with periods inserted between them. This can be done using the SUBSTR function and concatenation combined.

INITIALS = SUBSTR(NAME,1,1) || '.' || SUBSTR(NAME,2,1) || '.';

In this statement each letter of the initials is extracted and concatenated with the period.

    Finally let's ask how to take the name AJSIMPSON and store it in a second name field but with a space between the initials and surname. The second name field is declared as follows:

DCL NAME2 CHAR(10) INIT(' ');

SUBSTR(v,l,n)		
SUBSTR	–	is the function name
v	–	is the variable to which the function is referring
l	–	is the byte (character) location within the string
n	–	is the number of characters to be used

Fig. 4-9 *SUBSTR Function*

In this example we will use SUBSTR as a pseudo-variable. The initials are to be stored in positions 1 and 2 of NAME2. Position 3 is to remain blank and positions 4 to 10 will receive the surname giving the following result:

NAME2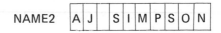

The following statements extract the data from NAME and assign it to NAME2.

SUBSTR(NAME2,1,2) = SUBSTR(NAME,1,2);
SUBSTR(NAME2,4,7) = SUBSTR(NAME,3,7);

The SUBSTR used on the left of the assignment symbol is a pseudo-variable because it defines a portion of the variable which receives the result of the operation. In this example two assignments are used to move initials and surname independently. This could have been done in one statement without a pseudo-variable by concatenating a blank between initials and surname.

Exercises

1. Write a series of assignment statements to assign the following data to the associated variable.

VARIABLE	DATA
a. DCL TØTAL FIXED(5,3);	000.00
b. DCL AMT FIXED(4,2);	2.5
c. DCL SWA BINARY(4);	1010
d. DCL NAME CHAR(20);	JACK SMITH
e. DCL FLD BIT(5);	00001

2. Referring to the declares in Exercise 1, what is the result of the following assignments?

   a. TØTAL = 4.23

   b. AMT = 0;

   c. SWA = 11B;

   d. NAME = 'ALØNZØ EDUARDØ ZACCARELLI';

   e. FLD = '001'B;

3. Given the following assignments, what is the result after each arithmetic statement has been executed in the sequence shown?

   A = 1.0;

   B = 2.0;

   N = 4;

   a. X = A+B;

   b. Y = A∗B;

   c. Z = A/B;

   d. W = X+Y–Z;

   e. X = X∗Y∗∗B/N;

   f. C = Y∗∗B∗∗2;

   g. C = (Y∗∗B)∗∗2;

   h. D = (((A∗2.0∗B)/N)∗∗3)–1.0

   i. K = –(N);

   j. N = –(K)∗–(N);

4. Each time a write routine is executed, we wish to add 2 to a LINE_CØUNT variable. Write a statement to accomplish this.

5. Write equivalent PL/I statements for the following algebraic expressions. (π = 3.1416)

   a. $h = a \cdot b$

   b. $a = b + c - d - e$

   c. $c = \dfrac{a \cdot b}{e}$

   d. $x = \dfrac{y + z}{w \cdot v}$

   e. $j = \dfrac{k + (l/n)}{m}$

   f. $r = \pi\, r^2$

   g. $v = \dfrac{4}{3}\,\pi\, r^3$

   h. $a = \pi\, r\sqrt{r^2 + h^2}$

   i. $e = a^{n^j}$

   j. $z = 1 - \left(\dfrac{x \cdot y - 1}{\pi r^2}\right)^n$

6. Write PL/I statements for the following algebraic expressions.

   a. $k = \sqrt{\dfrac{x + y}{z}}$

   b. $y = \sqrt{x^n}$

   c. $h = \sqrt{R^2 - r^2}$

   d. $x = \dfrac{-b + \sqrt{b^2 - 4ac}}{2a}$

   e. $C = \sin A + \sin B$

   f. $D = \sin A + \cos B$

   g. $AB = 2 \cos\left[\tfrac{1}{2}(a + b)\right] \cos\left[\tfrac{1}{2}(a - b)\right]$

   h. $\tan = \dfrac{\sin a}{\cos a}$

7. Concatenate the following groups of strings.

   a. A B   C D E
   b. JANUA   RY
   c. 23   00
   d. 1101   1011   Bits
   e. 12   13   71

8. Using an appropriate SUBSTR, concatenation, or both, produce the contents of B using data in field A. Additional literals may be used as necessary.

	A	B
a.	'10 27 77'	'27-10-77'
b.	'BOX 1500 NEW YORK'	'1500'
c.	'416-677-6810'	'4166776810'
d.	'102777'	'OCT.27,1977'

Programming Problems

1. An employee works 35 hours per week at a rate of $4.75 per hour. Write a program to declare and initial these values. Calculate a weekly salary. Print all of these values using

   PUT LIST(HOURS,RATE,SALARY);

2. A consumer buys 15 cassette tapes at a price of $4.95 each. Sales tax is paid at a rate of 7%. Write a program to calculate the cost of the tape, the amount of tax, and the total amount due for the purchase. Print each of these values using

   PUT LIST(QTY,UNIT,COST,TAX,AMOUNT);

3. Write a program to take the title THE PSYCHOLOGY OF COMPUTER PRO-GRAMMING, declared and initialized in one variable, and separate it into individual words. Print these on separate lines using a Put of the following form:

   PUT SKIP LIST(WORD);

Stream Input/Output

Two methods of getting data into a PL/I program have been established thus far. The first is using the initial attribute in a declare statement and the second method involves the use of an assignment statement.

These two methods are often not desirable for providing data to the program. The reason for this is that data often changes and can have many values. If this happens, it would be necessary to change the program each time new data are used.

For this reason data which is of a variable nature is usually read from data cards or some similar type of I/0 device. Refer to Fig. 1-7 on page 7 for the location of data cards in the job stream. Give particular attention to the fact that the data cards are outside of the PL/I program.

Get List

The simplest way to read information from a data card is with the GET LIST statement. Figure 5-1 shows the general format for the GET LIST statement.

```
1 2

   GET LIST (data-list);
```

Fig. 5-1

GET	Keyword which specifies an input operation.
LIST	Keyword which indicates the use of list directed data. List data is considered to be stream oriented. Stream organization does not recognize any boundaries of records. That is, a punched card is not processed as an 80-character record but rather as a continuous stream of data items.
(*data-list*)	This is composed of a list of data names defining the data to be read from a data card. Each name is separated by a comma and must appear in the same order as the data on the input device.

The keywords GET LIST are always specified whereas the data-list can differ depending upon the requirements of a specific program. Figure 5–2 shows a sample program using a GET statement to read a student card containing a student name, number, course number and grades for six different subjects.

```
01  SAMPLE: PROC OPTIONS(MAIN);
02  DCL NAME CHAR(15),
        NUMBER FIXED(8),
        COURSE FIXED(4),
        (GR1,GR2,GR3,GR4,GR5,GR6) FIXED(1);
03  DCL AVG FIXED(2,1);
04  GET LIST(NAME,NUMBER,COURSE,GR1,GR2,GR3,GR4,GR5,GR6);
05  AVG=(GR1+GR2+GR3+GR4+GR5+GR6)/6;
06  PUT LIST(NAME,NUMBER,COURSE,GR1,GR2,GR3,GR4,GR5,GR6,
        AVG);
07  END SAMPLE;
```

Fig. 5–2

The GET LIST (statement number 04) specifies that nine different data items are to be read from a data card and the values of this data are to be assigned to the variables named in the data list. A data card for this program may look like this:

'HARRY ØLINHØUSE' , 70073175 , 3701 , 3 , 4 , 2 , 3 , 1 , 2

Notice that the name, being a character string, is surrounded by apostrophes.

Each variable in the data card is separated by a comma surrounded by one or more blanks. After the GET LIST has been executed, each variable in the data list will have been assigned the related value from the data card. Thus NAME will contain the character string HARRY ØLINHØUSE, NUMBER will contain the value 70073175, and so on.

Since the variables GR1 through GR6 each contain a value, the average grade may now be calculated with an appropriate arithmetic statement.

The data card could also have been prepared without commas separating each item. Items may be separated by one or more blanks as follows:

'JAMES SCØTT' 71037952 3521 4 3 4 2 2 3

Because the character string is less than the 15 characters specified in the declare, blanks will be inserted in the low-order positions to make up the difference in length.

The primary advantage of a GET statement can be seen here. In the last example the data has been changed from the first data card. However nothing in the program needed to be changed in order to read a different data card.

In some cases a GET LIST may use only some of the data fields. In this case a null entry is made in the data card using an extra comma indicating the absence of a field.

GET LIST (W,X,Y,Z);

Data Card

| 38 , 33.75 , , 3.1 | Y missing |
| , 21.05 , 44 , 2.9 | W missing |

In these examples Y in the first case will be unchanged in the program while W, X, and Z will take on values 38, 33.75 and 3.1 respectively. The second example will cause X, Y, and Z to be changed leaving W unchanged.

Figure 5-2 shows a PUT LIST for statement number 06. Once data has been read by the program and then processed (average calculated), some printed output is desired to show the results. A PUT LIST statement is used to place the data on the printer.

Put List

The PUT LIST statement causes data to be written on an output device, usually a printer. Its general format is similar to the GET LIST and is shown in Fig. 5-3.

| 1 | 2 |

PUT LIST (*data-list*);

Fig. 5-3

PUT   Keyword which specifies an output opera-
                                 tion.

LIST   Keyword. See GET LIST.

(*data-list*)   Same rules as for GET LIST.

Using the same approach as for a GET LIST, the PUT LIST in Fig. 5-2 is

PUT LIST (NAME,NUMBER,CØURSE,GR1,GR2,
GR3,GR4,GR5,GR6,AVG);

This statement would cause output to appear on the printer as follows:

HARRY ØLINHØUSE 70073175 3701 3 4 2 3 1 2 2.5

The last figure (2.5) is the value calculated by the program for AVG.

In this example it is not clear which value represents each variable. Usually
a programmer is expected to identify output with some kind of description or
heading. To do this a character string may also be included in the PUT LIST.
The characters from the string will be printed to identify each output value. This
principle is demonstrated in Fig. 5-4.

```
01  PAYROLL:PROC OPTIONS(MAIN);
02  DCL PAYNO FIXED(6),
        HRS FIXED(3),
        RATE FIXED(4,2),
        AMT FIXED(6,2);
03  GET LIST(PAYNO,HRS,RATE);
04  AMT = HRS*RATE;
05  PUT LIST('PAYROLL NUMBER',PAYNO,'HOURS',HRS,
            'HOURLY RATE',RATE,'GROSS AMOUNT',AMT);
06  END;
```

Fig. 5-4 *Payroll Program*

In this program an employee's payroll number, the number of hours
worked, and the hourly rate is read from a data card by statement number 03.

Gross salary is computed in statement 04 and printed with the input data in statement 05. Note the additional descriptive information supplied to make the output more readable. Given the following input data for the above program

836010 35 4.00

the output would be

PAYROLL NUMBER   836010   HOURS   35   HOURLY RATE   4.00
GROSS AMOUNT   140.00

     The output from this program is a definite improvement over the previous one. Each value has a description which tells what the number represents. However the organization of the output across the page is not as esthetic as it might be. This could be improved by printing each value on a separate line. To do this requires a new option in the general format PUT LIST (Fig. 5-5).

---

1 2

   PUT SKIP LIST (data list);
   PUT SKIP(n) LIST (data list);

Fig. 5-5 *SKIP Option*

     The SKIP option instructs the program to skip the printer to the next line before printing the data list. SKIP(n) allows skipping of 0, 1, 2, or 3 lines prior to printing. For example

PUT SKIP LIST(NUM);

will skip one line prior to printing.

PUT SKIP(1) LIST (NUM);

does exactly the same thing. The statement

PUT SKIP(2) LIST(NUM);

will skip two lines before printing. This can sometimes be misleading if previous data had been printed. For instance, the statements

NUM = 1234;
PUT LIST('NUMBER');
PUT SKIP(2) LIST(NUM);

would print

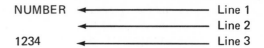

NUMBER	Line 1
	Line 2
1234	Line 3

This leaves only 1 line between NUMBER and 1234. The reason is the printer was still at line 1 following the first PUT. The SKIP(2) causes it to move down two lines to line 3 thus leaving only one blank line.

The SKIP(0) causes the printer to begin again at print position one of the same line. This is generally only useful for underlining and overprinting.

The program from Fig. 5-4 is now rewritten in Fig. 5-6 showing the new output using the SKIP option.

```
01  PAYROLL:PROC OPTIONS(MAIN);
02  DCL PAYNO FIXED(6),
        HRS FIXED(3),
        RATE FIXED(4,2),
        AMT FIXED(6,2);
03  GET LIST(PAYNO,HRS,RATE);
04  AMT = HRS*RATE;
05  PUT SKIP LIST('PAYROLL NUMBER',PAYNO);
06  PUT SKIP LIST('HOURS=',HRS);
07  PUT SKIP LIST('HOURLY RATE',RATE);
08  PUT SKIP LIST('GROSS AMOUNT=',AMT);
09  END;
```

PAYROLL NUMBER	836010
HOURS=	35
HOURLY RATE	4.00
GROSS AMOUNT=	140.00

Fig. 5-6

The SKIP may also be used alone if there is no data to be printed at the time.

PUT SKIP;	Skips 1 line
PUT SKIP(3);	Skips 3 lines

Another option available is

> PUT PAGE;
> PUT PAGE LIST(data-list);

This causes the printer to skip to the first line of a new page. This is useful for ensuring a report begins on a clean page and doesn't follow directly after other output. Also available is the form

> PUT LINE(n);
> PUT LINE(n) LIST(data-list);

This form spaces the printer to a specific line number on the page. Lines are counted from the top of the page beginning at 1 and increasing by increments of one. The statement

> PUT LINE(17) LIST(NUM);

will cause the contents of the variable NUM to be printed on the 17th line of the page.

The primary disadvantage of the GET LIST and PUT LIST statements is that the programmer has very little direct control over selecting data from given locations in the input record. On printed output the programmer cannot define precisely where the output data is to appear on a line or page. Thus the list oriented statements are usually limited to simple forms of input and output. More complex I/0 can be manipulated with greater dexterity using a GET EDIT or PUT EDIT statement.

Get Edit

A GET EDIT statement is very similar in appearance and use to a GET LIST. It consists of two keywords followed by a data list and is used for stream input data. Following the data list is a format list which was not used in the LIST oriented statement. The format list defines the type and relative location of data to be read. The general format of the GET EDIT statement is shown in Fig. 5-7.

1│ 2

│ GET EDIT (*data list*) (*format list*);

Fig. 5-7

GET	Keyword specifying an input operation.
EDIT	Keyword which indicates the use of edit directed data.
(*data list*)	One or more variables which are to receive values from an input device. Each name is separated by a comma and must appear in the same order as the data in the input stream.
(*format list*)	One or more format items (see below). Each item in the data list will have a corresponding item in the format list. If there are fewer format items than data items, the following format item is taken from the beginning of the list. There are three types of format items: data, control, and remote format items.
;	Semicolon used to terminate statement.

Data Format Items

Each data format item is associated with a data item and specifies how many characters or digits that data item is composed of and the relative location of that item in the input stream. There are four data format items permitted in a GET EDIT. Their general format is shown in Fig. 5-8.

F (*w,d*)	Fixed Point
E (*w,d*)	Floating Point
A (*w*)	Character String
B (*w*)	Bit String

Fig. 5-8 *Data Format Items*

The *w* represents the number of characters in the width of the field and *d* the number of digits to the right of the decimal point. A card containing a five digit account number in columns 1-5, a customer name in columns 6-15 and an amount in columns 16-20 might look like this

23701JACK JØNES27.59

This card could not be read using a GET LIST since no blanks or commas separate the fields. However, this is done quite easily with the following:

GET EDIT (ACCØUNT,NAME, AMØUNT)
(F(5,0),A(10),F(5,2));

The first format item F(5,0) relates to the first data item ACCØUNT and causes the first five digits from the data file to be transferred to ACCØUNT. A(10) relates to NAME and F(5,2) relates to AMØUNT. Since there are no decimals in the first field, the first format item could be written as F(5) giving identical results. It is not essential to punch a decimal point in the data card as was done for AMØUNT. Without this decimal the card might look like this:

23701JACK JØNES02759

In this example, the high-order zero is inserted to make up the difference in the field length. This column could also be blank:

23701JACK JØNES 2759

In any event it is essential that the data be right-adjusted in the field (columns 16–20). The same GET EDIT may be used for either of these data cards. Also notice that the character string JACK JØNES is not contained within apostrophes as was the case with list-oriented data. For edit-oriented data, the format item A(w) identifies the character string.

When a data card contains a series of fields of identical format and precision it is unnecessary to write a data format item for each. Suppose you had this data card:

27.750 31.695 63.011 49.712

This card contains four decimal numbers, each with a high-order blank in the field. An appropriate GET EDIT might be

GET EDIT (NUMA,NUMB,NUMC,NUMD)(F(7,3));

This would be equivalent to writing

GET EDIT (NUMA,NUMB,NUMC,NUMD)
(F(7,3),F(7,3),F(7,3),F(7,3));

Any combination of multiple data can use this same approach as long as they are repeated consistently. Given

BØB37TØM51JØE33

the following GET EDIT may be used

GET EDIT(NAME1,NUM1,NAME2,NUM2,
NAME3,NUM3)(A(3),F(2));

Effectively, the two format items will each be used three times, thus relating to all six data names.

Iteration Factor

The Optimizer compiler allows an iteration factor to be used in a format listed to represent a reoccurrence of the same format. For instance

GET EDIT (NUM1,NUM2) (2 F(7,3));

indicates that two fixed numbers containing 7 digits each are to be read. A group of items may also be repeated with the iteration factor as follows:

GET EDIT (NUM1,NAME1,NUM2,NAME2)
(2(F(5),X(1),A(10)));

This reads a value of five digits for NUM1 followed by a space (1 card column) and then a 10-character name. NUM2 follows immediately using F(5). A space occurs again and the second 10-character name is read.

Another useful variation allows for an expression in the format. A format item such as A(I) reserves I columns for the field referenced by the A format. Prior to this use I must be given a value. For example

I = 12;
GET EDIT (NAME) (A(I));

causes a 12-character name to be read.

GET EDIT(NAME) (A(I+2));

would cause a name of 14 characters to be read providing I was still the value 12.

Control Format Items

Data cards are not always as nicely organized as the preceding examples have shown. For instance each field may be separated by a given number of unused or blank columns giving the format:

COLUMNS	DATA NAME	VALUE
1–5	Account Number	23701
6–10	blank	
11–20	Customer Name	JACK JØNES
21–26	blank	
27–31	Amount (2 decimal)	02759

This card could be read by treating each blank field as alphanumeric data and using A format characters. However, this approach does mean declaring each blank field which requires additional storage space. Using the appropriate Fig. 5-9, control format item helps to eliminate this problem.

X(w)   w = width of data to be spaced over

CØLUMN(p)   p = position or card column to space to

SKIP(w)   w = 1, skip one card or record
                                            2, skip two cards or records
                                            3, skip three cards or records
                                            if w is omitted, 1 is assumed.

Fig. 5-9 *Control Format Items*

The GET for reading the data card could be written

GET EDIT(ACT, NAME,AMT)(F(5),X(5),
A(10),X(6),F(5,2));

As before, the F(5) takes the first five columns of data and assigns it to the data name ACT. The next five columns are spaced over as a result of the X(5) control format item. If there had been data in columns 6-10 this data would have been ignored. There is no data name associated with the X control format item. Similarly the next X control X(6) causes six columns from 21-26 to be spaced over.

If an X control format item is written at the end of the format list, it is ignored. For example, suppose the program is to read more than one data card. Since GET EDIT is a stream oriented I/0 statement, the second time it is executed the program will attempt to read ACT from columns 32-36 in the original card. The reason is that the record (card) contains 80 columns of data and since it is stream, the next record of 31 characters would still appear within the 80-character card. Normally this is not desirable since it presents keypunching problems. Therefore the second record would be in a second card again in columns 1-31.

This can be done by reading all 80 columns of each card in the GET EDIT statement. If we were to write

GET EDIT (ACT,NAME,AMT)(F(5),X(5),
A(10),X(6),F(5,2),X(39));

the X(39) is intended to account for the unused columns remaining in the data card. However, as stated earlier since this is the last format item it will be ignored. To get around this a DUMMY field is declared as CHAR(1) and this will be used as the last data item in the card as follows:

```
GET EDIT (ACT,NAME,AMT,DUMMY)(F(5),
          X(5),A(10),X(6),F(5,2),X(48),A(1));
```

Since the DUMMY requires one character, the X control format item is reduced by one. Thus the sum of all format items is 80, the length of the card, and the last format item is not X.

The X control format item may be replaced by CØLUMN. However, this will result in less efficient coding. This is done as follows:

```
GET EDIT (ACT,NAME,AMT)(CØLUMN(1),F(5),CØLUMN(11),
          A(10),CØLUMN(27),F(5,2));
```

In this example the first format item CØLUMN(1) causes data to be taken beginning with the first column of the record. NAME will be taken beginning with column 11. When the GET is executed a second time, reading will begin at column 1 in the next data card.

Input records may also be skipped using the SKIP format item. For example the statement

```
GET EDIT(X,Y,Z)(F(6,3),SKIP,F(5,2),SKIP,F(3));
```

causes X, a field of 6 digits, to be read from the first card, Y, a field of 5 digits, to be read from the second card and Z, a field of 3 digits, to be read from a third card.

This method may also be applied to the problem of unused columns in a data card. This is used instead of the column or dummy field approach.

```
GET EDIT(ACT,NAME,AMT) (SKIP,F(5),X(5),A(10),X(6),F(5,2));
```

The SKIP causes the GET EDIT to skip over the remaining fields of the previous card and begin in column 1 of the next card. In the optimizer, the SKIP is ignored on the first GET but on each subsequent GET the remaining card columns are passed over. In PL/C the first card will be skipped which is not desirable. This can be corrected by preceding the data cards with a blank card.

Remote Format Item

The remote format item consists of the format character R followed by the label of the format list. The format list may then be written separately anywhere in the program. This makes it possible for one format list to be used by several GET statements or for a GET statement to select one of a number of format lists. The former is demonstrated by the following example:

GET EDIT (NAME1,ADDRESS1)(R(LIST));

GET EDIT (NAME2,ADDRESS2)(R(LIST));

LIST: FØRMAT(A(20),A(60));

When each GET EDIT is used, the format list is found by going to the remote list named LIST. At this symbolic location the format list is identified by its label and the keyword FØRMAT. The format list is then written as usual.

Put Edit

The PUT EDIT is similar in format to the GET EDIT except, of course, that it is used to produce output. Usually in the basic form it is used to produce printed output. The print line created may be either 120 or 132 characters per line depending on the printer used. Figure 5-10 shows the general format for the PUT EDIT statement.

---

1 2

PUT EDIT*(data list)(format list)*;

Fig. 5-10

PUT	Keyword specifying an output operation.
EDIT	Keyword specifying the use of edit directed data.
(data list)	List of variables to be transferred to an output device.
(format list)	Format items relating to the data items. As with the GET EDIT there are data, control, and remote format items.
;	Semicolon used to terminate the statement.

Data Format Items

These are the same format items as described for the GET EDIT. They are

F (w,d)	Fixed Point
E (w,d)	Floating Point
A(w)	Character String
B(w)	Bit String

The only consideration here is that *w* refers to the number of print positions occupied by the field.

Control Format Items

These perform the same function as for input except as indicated in Fig. 5-11.

PAGE	Causes control to skip to the top of a new page.
SKIP(*w*)	*w* can be any value from 0 to 3 specifying the number of lines to be skipped.
LINE(*w*)	Causes control to skip to the line specified. A *w* less than the present print line should not be specified.
CØLUMN(*p*)	Used in the same way as for input data.
X(*w*)	Same as for input.

Fig. 5-11

Remote Format Item

The remote format item functions the same for a PUT EDIT as for a GET EDIT. In rare cases the same format may be used for both the GET and PUT EDIT, but usually input and output requirements are different, particularly when the output is a printed line.

The Payroll Program from Fig. 5-4 is now rewritten in Fig. 5-12 using the GET EDIT and PUT EDIT statements.

```
1  PAYROLL:PROC OPTIONS(MAIN);
2  DCL PAYNO FIXED(6),
       HRS FIXED(3),
       RATE FIXED(4,2),
       AMT FIXED(6,2);
3  PUT EDIT('PAYROLL REPORT','PAYROLL NUMBER',
       'HOURS','HOURLY RATE','GROSS AMOUNT')
       (PAGE,X(16),A(14),SKIP(2),A(14),X(2),
       A(5),X(2),A(11),X(2),A(12));
4  GET EDIT(PAYNO,HRS,RATE)(F(6),F(3),F(4,2));
5  AMT=HRS*RATE;
```

```
6  PUT EDIT(PAYNO,HRS,RATE,AMT) (SKIP(2),X(4),
        F(6),X(6),F(3),X(7),F(5,2),X(7),F(7,2));
7  END;
```

Fig. 5-12

Given input data 8360100350400, the output would be:

```
                    PAYROLL REPORT
PAYROLL NUMBER   HOURS  HOURLY RATE   GROSS AMOUNT
    836010         35      4.00          140.00
```

Notice the format item for AMT is F(7,2) whereas the declare is FIXED(6,2). The extra digit compensates for the extra print position required for the decimal point. In the above example the extra position was not used, therefore AMT was preceded by a leading blank.

The use of PAGE,SKIP,X and the data format items helps to create a more readable report with a more pleasing appearance.

As discussed with the PUT LIST statement the PAGE, SKIP, and LINE attributes may be used directly in a PUT statement without the necessity for printing data at the time. This is also valid for use with the PUT EDIT as follows:

```
PUT PAGE;
PUT SKIP(n);
PUT LINE(n);
```


File Declaration—D-LEVEL AND OPTIMIZER COMPILERS

GET and PUT statements, as discussed so far, always refer to the two standard system files. The system names for these files are SYSIPT, usually a card reader, and SYSLST, usually a printer. Many PL/I programs require the use of additional files such as magnetic tapes and magnetic disks.

When files other than the standard system files are required in a program they must be declared using a file declaration. Standard system files may also be declared if desired. Figure 5-13 shows the attributes used when declaring stream input or output files. A description of each of these file attributes follows:

1. The *filename* consists of 1-6 alphanumeric characters. The first character must be alphabetic. This name identifies the file to be used. Examples of file names are FILEA,FILE4,REPØRT,UPDATE, etc. Even though UP-DATE is a keyword used in file declaration it is not reserved. It is only recognized as a keyword when taken in the context of a declare.

2. The attribute FILE is a keyword which indicates a file declaration. Since this attribute defaults in a declare it is not essential that it be used.

3. The STREAM attribute is a keyword indicating a stream-oriented file. An alternate to STREAM is RECØRD which is discussed in Chapters 9 and 10.

4. The INPUT or ØUTPUT attribute indicates whether an input or output file respectively is being declared.

5. The attribute PRINT is a keyword specifying that ultimately this file is to be printed although it may not be printed directly. With this attribute the PAGE,LINE, and SKIP options may be used in the PUT statement and PAGESIZE may be used in the ØPEN statement. The PRINT attribute requires that the first byte of the output be reserved for printer control information. Thus the print line should be 1 byte longer than the required output. If the print line is 120 bytes, then the block size should be 121 bytes. If the line is 132 bytes, then the block size is 133 bytes. This control character is set by the PAGE, LINE, and SKIP options.

6. ENVIRØNMENT(is a keyword specifying the environment section is to follow. It may be abbreviated to ENV(if desired.

7. MEDIUM(is a keyword specifying the I/O medium being used. This relates to the hardware device associated with the file declare.

8. The SYSIPT,SYSPCH,SYSLST and SYS*nnn* attributes specify the system name for the I/O device being used. In the case of SYS*nnn* the value *nnn* may be in the range 000-222. Since this may vary from one installation to another, it is best to check with your computer center for the permitted range.

9. The 2501|2520|2540|1442) attributes supply the machine type of the card reader punch unit being used. Choose one of these numbers depending upon the hardware used in your installation.

10. The 1403|1404|1443|1445) attributes supply the machine type of the printer being used. Choose one of these. 2400) is used for Magnetic Tape and 2311|2314|3340|2321) are used for Direct Access Storage Devices.

11. The F(*block size*) attribute specifies the number of bytes in a data record. For a card it might be F(80) for a printer F(132) when not PRINT, and for a printer using the PRINT attribute F(133) could be used. In the optimizer, the entries used are F BLKSIZE(80) or F BLKSIZE(133).

12. The BUFFERS(1) attribute specifies the use of one I/O area. If it is not specified, it is a default unless the BUFFERS(2) attribute is used. This specifies the use of two I/O areas for greater I/O efficiency. When BUFFERS(2) is specified BUFFERS(1) is not.

13. The attribute LEAVE is used only for tape files. When used the tape file is not rewound at open or close time. This could be used when processing multifile reels of tape.

14. NØLABEL specifies that no labels will be processed for tape files. The programmer may, however, create and process his own labels. In this case the program itself would have a label processing routine.

15. The NØTAPEMK attribute prevents a leading tapemark from being written ahead of data records on unlabeled (NOLABEL) tape files. A tapemark is a magnetic character used by the operating system.

16. When VERIFY is used for DASD, a read-check after each write operation will occur. This ensures the validity of the data just written.

17. CØNSECUTIVE indicates that each logical record physically succeeds the previous logical record. Normally this is the case on all card readers, punches, printers, and magnetic tapes.

18. A closing bracket ends the Declare statement.

A card input file located at SYS004 using a 2501 reader is declared demonstrating how the attributes are selected from Fig. 5-13.

1│2

DCL CARD FILE STREAM INPUT

   ENVIRØNMENT(MEDIUM(SYS004,2501)F(80)

   BUFFERS(1) CØNSECUTIVE);

The name CARD is chosen by the programmer. Normally any name is acceptable providing it conforms to the rules for file names. This declare could be written as follows utilizing the default attributes.

1│2

 │ DCL CARD INPUT ENV(MEDIUM(SYS004,2501)F(80));

The same declare in the optimizer would be

FILE TYPE	INPUT			OUTPUT NOT PRINT			OUTPUT PRINT		
ATTRIBUTES	CARD	TAPE	DASD	CARD/PRINTER	TAPE	DASD	PRINTER	TAPE	DASD
filename	S	S	S	S	S	S	S	S	S
FILE	D	D	D	D	D	D	D	D	D
STREAM	D	D	D	D	D	D	D	D	D
INPUT	S	S	S						
ØUTPUT				S	S	S	D	D	D
PRINT							S	S	S
ENVIRØNMENT(	S	S	S	S	S	S	S	S	S
MEDIUM(	S	S	S	S	S	S	S	S	S
SYSIPT,	C	C	C						
SYSPCH,				C	C	C			
SYSLST,				C	C	C	C	C	C
SYSnnn,	C	C	C	C	C	C	C	C	C
2501|2520|2540|1442)	S			C					
1403|1404|1443|1445)				C			S		
2400)		S			S			S	
2311|2314|3340|2321)			S			S			S
F (*blocksize*)	S	S	S	S	S	S	S	S	S
BUFFERS (1)	D	D	D	D	D	D	D	D	D
BUFFERS (2)	O	O	O	O	O	O	O	O	O
LEAVE		O			O			O	
NØLABEL		O			O			O	
NØTAPEMK					O			O	
VERIFY						O			O
CØNSECUTIVE	D	D	D	D	D	D	D	D	D
)	S	S	S	S	S	S	S	S	S

S — Specify this attribute
O — Optional attribute
D — Default if not specified
C — Choose one of these attributes

Fig. 5-13 *Stream File Declaration*

```
1 2
  DCL CARD INPUT ENV( MEDIUM(SYS004,2501) F BLKSIZE(80));
```

Similarly a 2311 disk output file producing 100-byte records on SYS000 file name FILEA may be declared as follows:

```
1 2
  DCL FILEA ØUTPUT ENV(MEDIUM(SYS000,2311)
     F(100) BUFFERS(2) VERIFY);
```

In this example BUFFERS(2) is used for output efficiency. This attribute will require additional storage space for the output as opposed to BUFFERS(1). VERIFY is used to ensure accuracy of the output. This is a compromise since it reduces I/O efficiency as each record written must also be read for verification. Usually disk output is accurate and the necessity for VERIFY is debatable.

Open

When a file has been explicitly declared it is necessary to ØPEN that file prior to any GET statement. The ØPEN statement makes the file available to the PL/I program. The general format for the ØPEN is shown in Fig. 5-14.

```
1 2
  ØPEN FILE(filename),FILE(filename), - - -;
```

Fig. 5-14

Using this format the files in the preceding examples could be opened as follows:

```
1 2
  ØPEN FILE(CARD),FILE(FILEA);
```

For print output files a standard page size is established which specifies how many lines can be printed on a page of output. This standard size applies only to a given installation. If the size is not valid for a given program it may be changed by the PAGESIZE(*n*) option in the ØPEN statement. Thus if a page of 75 lines were required, the ØPEN for the printer would look like

---

| 1 | 2 |

ØPEN FILE(REPØRT)PAGESIZE(75);

The maximum value of *n* for PAGESIZE(*n*) is 255. When the program terminates the page size returns to its original value.

Close

When a file has been completely processed and there is no longer any need for this file, it must be closed prior to termination of the program. The general format appears in Fig. 5-15.

| 1 | 2 |

CLØSE FILE(*filename*)FILE(*filename*),---;

Fig. 5-15

The preceding files would be closed as follows:

| 1 | 2 |

CLØSE FILE(CARD),FILE(FILEA),FILE(REPØRT);

File Attribute in Get and Put

When the input or output files have been explicitly declared, the file name used must appear in the GET or PUT statement. This serves to identify the particular file required for the given I/O operation. The general formats using file name are shown in Fig. 5-16.

```
1 2

   GET FILE(filename) LIST (datalist);

   GET FILE(filename) EDIT (data list)(format list);

   PUT FILE(filename) LIST (data list);

   PUT FILE(filename) EDIT (data list)(format list);
```

Fig. 5-16

An example of the use of this format for a disk output file might be:

```
1 2

   PUT FILE(FILEA)EDIT(A,B,C)(F(7),F(10,2),A(83));
```

The only difference from previous understanding of the PUT is the inclusion of the FILE(filename) attribute. All other attributes remain the same.

On Endfile

The endfile statement permits the programmer to recognize when all records in a file have been exhausted and the end of that file has been reached. Figure 5-17 shows the general format.

```
1 2

   ØN ENDFILE(filename) action;
```

Fig. 5-17

The ENDFILE statement controls the orderly termination of the program. This may involve such activities as printing of totals, closing files and stopping the program.

```
1 2

  ON ENDFILE (CARD) BEGIN;

    CLOSE FILE(CARD),FILE(PRINT);

    STOP;

    END;
```

Normally the ENDFILE statement appears after the OPEN statement for the file involved. It needs to be executed only once to establish the action to be taken upon reaching end of file.

Get String

The GET STRING statement is a very useful tool which is used to transmit data internally within the program. It functions in a way similar to the GET EDIT except that instead of data coming from an input device it is taken from a character string variable in the program. The general format is shown in Fig. 5-18.

```
1 2

  GET STRING(variable)EDIT(data list)(format list);
```

Fig. 5-18

GET STRING	Are keywords which identify the statement type.
(*variable*)	Is a variable name which contains the character string data to be operated upon.
EDIT(*data list*)(*format list*)	Is the same form used in the GET EDIT statement.

Suppose we have a character string field containing a Part Number, Stock Location, and Description. This field is declared as DCL DATA CHAR(37); where the first 10 bytes contain the part number, the next seven contain stock location (row, shelf, bin) and the last 20 bytes contain the description.

The program is to take this information from DATA and assign the appropriate bytes to the following declared variables

```
DCL  PART   FIXED  (10),
     RØW    FIXED  ( 3),
     SHELF  FIXED  ( 2),
     BIN    FIXED  ( 2),
     DESC   CHAR   (20);
```

This may be done simply with the GET STRING by writing

```
GET STRING(DATA)EDIT(PART,RØW,SHELF,BIN,DESC)
           (F(10),F(3),2F(2),A(20));
```

This statement causes data to be taken from the character string DATA and assigns it to the variables PART,RØW,SHELF,BIN, and DESC respectively. The format list is used to specify the relative positions of the data items within DATA.

Another common application for the GET STRING is for processing files which contain records of two or more formats. Suppose we are reading data cards which were punched from sales invoices. They could consist of two different card formats. The first might contain information related to the customer. The second contains data relating to the purchase. Thus each customer's purchase would be recorded using one "customer" card followed by any number of "purchase" cards. The number of the "purchase" cards depends upon the number of items bought by the customer. The formats for these cards is as follows.

Customer Card Format

1–7	Invoice Number
8–12	Customer Number
13–25	Name
26–40	Address
41–46	Date of Purchase
49	Credit Code
50	Card Code "1"

Purchase Card Format

1–7	Invoice Number
8–15	Part Number
16–20	Quantity
21–27	Unit Cost
28–35	Total Cost
50	Card Code "2"

Figure 5-19 shows an example of how the GET STRING might be used to read data of this type. The main problem here is that we don't know in advance which card will be read. Thus the GET EDIT deals with the data which is common to both formats, INVØICE and CØDE. The other data is treated as a character string and placed in the variable DETAIL.

```
DCL INVØICE FIXED (7),
       DETAIL CHAR (42),
       CØDE CHAR (1),
       UNUSED CHAR (1);

DCL CUSTØMER FIXED (5),
       NAME CHAR (13),
       ADR CHAR (15),
       DATE FIXED (6),
       CREDIT FIXED (1);

DCL PART FIXED (8),
       QTY FIXED (5),
       UNIT FIXED (7,2),
       TØTAL FIXED (8,2);
            .
            .
            .

GET EDIT(INVØICE,DETAIL,CØDE,UNUSED)
          (F(7),A(42),A(1),X(29),A(1));

IF CODE = '1' THEN DO;
     GET STRING(DETAIL)EDIT(CUSTOMER,NAME,ADR,DATE,CREDIT)
                    (F(5),A(13),A(15),F(6),X(2),F(1));
            .
            .
     END;  .
            ELSE DO;
     GET STRING(DETAIL)EDIT(PART,QTY,UNIT,TOTAL)
                    (F(8),F(5),F(7,2),F(8,2));
            .
            .
            .
     END;
```

Fig. 5-19

An IF statement (see Chapter 6) is used to determine the type of card read. If a code '1' was read, the first GET STRING is executed. This gets the data from DETAIL and places it in CUSTØMER,NAME,ADR,DATE, and CREDIT which is the order in which this information appears in DETAIL. If the code read was a '2,' a GET STRING extracts the information for the purchase card format and assigns it to the appropriate variables.

Put String

The PUT STRING statement functions in a similar way to the GET STRING. The main difference is that data is taken from various variables and placed together in one character string variable. The general format is shown in Fig. 5–20.

```
1 2

  PUT STRING(variable)EDIT(data list)(format list);
```

Fig. 5–20

PUT STRING	Are keywords which identify the statement type.
(*variable*)	Is the name of the character string variable which is to receive the data.
EDIT(*data list*)(*format list*)	Is the same form used in the PUT EDIT statement.

The use of the PUT STRING may be described simply with the following example.

```
DCL NUMBER FIXED (4),
    STREET CHAR (15),
    CITY CHAR (10),
    ZIP FIXED (5);
DCL ADDRESS CHAR (34);
PUT STRING(ADDRESS)EDIT(NUMBER,STREET,CITY,ZIP)
        (F(4),A(15),A(10),F(5));
```

Here are four data items NUMBER,STREET,CITY and ZIP that we want to place together into one field called ADDRESS. This is exactly what the

PUT STRING does. Each field is assigned to ADDRESS in the order shown and will occupy the number of bytes defined by the format list.

Exercises

1. Write appropriate GET LIST statements for the following data cards.

    a. ⌐ 'NAME','JACKSØN',3600

    b. ⌐ 365 , 47.59 , 'E.59TH STREET'

    c. ⌐ 735101 258 01.79 'PULLEY WHEEL'

    d. ⌐ 37,49,,68,

    e. ⌐ ,,18.759

2. Write PUT LIST statements for the data read in Exercise 1.

3. Write GET EDIT statements for the following data.
    a. Col 1-5   Product Code (Numeric)
           6-12   Inventory Number
          13-17   Unit Cost
          18-35   Description

        e.g. ⌐ 23500890511105.68 ROTARY SAW BLADE

    b.   1-7   Account Number
           8   Unused
          9-11   Branch
           12   Unused
         13-18   Date Opened
         19-20   Unused
         21-26   Balance (In dollars and cents)
         27-30   Unused
         31-50   Customer Name

        e.g. ⌐ 0375101 200 072171 002350 J.J. RIVERS

4. a. Write PUT EDIT for the preceding data ensuring at least one space between each data item on printout.

   b. Write PUT EDIT to create headings at the top of a page for the preceding data.

5. Write file declares for the file used in Exercise 3 and 4. The card reader is a 2501 and the printer a 1403.

6. Write ØPEN and CLØSE statements for the files declared in 5. Write an ON ENDFILE for the input file.

Programming Problems

1. Prepare a data card containing your name and address. Write a program to read and print the card.

2. The volume of a cube is computed by the formula $V = L \cdot W \cdot D$. Write a program to read these three values (L,W,D) from one data card. Compute volume and print V,L,W, and D with the following headings.

```
LENGTH   WIDTH   DEPTH   VOLUME
  10        5       7       350
```

3. The volume of a sphere is computed by the formula $4\pi R^3/3$—the surface area by $4\pi R^2$. Read R from a data card, compute, and print volume and area for radius R.

```
GIVEN THE RADIUS 13
THE VOLUME IS 9202.77
THE AREA IS 2123.72
```

4. Simple interest is found with the formula I = Prt where I = interest(dollars and cents), P = principal, r = rate(percent) and t = time(years). If $5000 is borrowed over a period of 3 years at a rate of 13%, write a program to calculate the interest paid during that time. Use the following card format.

1-6 Principal

7-8 Rate

9-10 Years

5. A salesman receives a basic income plus a commission based on 10 percent of his total sales. Using the following data card format compute his gross and net salary using Tax Percent for deduction of income tax. Print all input and computed data under appropriate headings.

Column   1-5   Salesman Number

         6-20   Name

         21-26 Sales Amount

         27-31 Basic Salary

         32-34 Tax Percent

6. Tom Brown works five days of the week at the regular rate. But on Saturdays he is paid overtime at 1½ times the regular rate. Read the following card and produce the output shown.

1 - 20   Name

21 - 22 Monday Hours

23 - 24 Tuesday ''

25 - 26 Wednesday ''

27 - 28 Thursday ''

29 - 30 Friday   ''

31 - 32 Saturday ''

33 - 36 Rate per Hour

NAME	HOURS WORKED	OVERTIME HOURS	REGULAR RATE	OVERTIME RATE	GROSS SALARY
TOM BROWN	3 7	5	4 . 0 0	6 . 0 0	1 7 8 . 0 0

7. The economic order quantity for a part is given by the formula:

$$EOQ = \sqrt{\frac{2dc}{us}}$$

where d is the demand in units

      c is the cost of placing an order

      u is the unit cost of the part

      s is the cost of storing the item in stock

Write a program to calculate EOQ using the following input format:

1 - 3   Demand

4 - 7   Order Cost

8 - 12   Unit Cost

13 - 16 Storage Cost

Print the following output:

DEMAND	ORDER COST	UNIT COST	STORAGE COST	EOQ
XXX	XX.XX	XXX.XX	XX.XX	XXX

8. Three basic costs are involved in producing a product. The first being material cost, the second labor and the third overhead. Material is a fixed cost which appears in card 1 as follows:

1-7   Product Number

9   Card Number (1)

11-17 Material Cost (3 decimal positions)

Labor cost depends upon the number of hours worked at a given hourly rate. This appears in card 2:

1-7   Product Number

9   Card Number (2)

11-14 Hours

15-19 Hourly Rate

Overhead is also based on the number of hours worked from card 2 at a given overhead rate from card 3:

1–7	Product Number
9	Card Number (3)
15–19	Overhead Rate

Write a program to read these cards and produce the following report:

```
              PRODUCT COST SUMMARY

PRODUCT  MATERIAL   HOURS   LABOR  OVERHEAD  OVERHEAD
NUMBER     COST    WORKED   COST     RATE      COST
XXXXXXX XXXX.XXX    XXXX   XXX.XX   XXXX.XX   XXXX.XX


           TOTAL PRODUCT COST XXXXX.XXX
```

6

Problem Solving and Statement Control

Top Down Development

As problems become larger and more complex it is important to plan the program logic prior to writing the PL/I coding. This allows the programmer to concentrate on problem solving rather than the programming language. After a solution has been prepared the primary effort is in writing correct PL/I code. The method of problem solving used in this book is top down development which leads quite naturally to structured programming techniques.

Applying the techniques described here will help the programmer to reduce the number of errors written, make programs easier to read and understand, simplify logic, and make debugging easier.

The term *top down development* refers to the method of problem solving used prior to program coding. It consists of stating the solution to a problem first in quite general terms. This is the top level. Then each top level statement is broken down into further detail. These statements are further broken down until no more detail is necessary.

Fig. 6-1 *Top Down Development*

The Product Cost Summary from Chapter 5 might be developed as shown in Figs. 6–2 to 6–4.

1. Print Headings

2. Read Data

3. Calculate Costs

4. Print Detail

5. Print Total

6. Stop

Fig. 6-2 *Product Cost Summary Top Level*

Figure 6–2 shows how the top level solution to the problem might be stated. Notice that each entry made is quite simple and states in general terms what is to be done. It is important at this stage that the sequence of events be logically correct.

Now each entry that can be expanded is developed to a more detail level as shown in Fig. 6–3.

1.1   Print Heading Line 1

1.2   Pring Heading Line 2

1.3   Print Heading Line 3

3.1   Labor Cost is Hours times Labor Rate

3.2   Overhead Cost is Hours time Overhead Rate

3.3   Total Cost is Material Cost plus Labor Cost plus Overhead Cost

Fig. 6-3

In this problem only levels 1 and 3 need to be developed further. In fact, since level 1 is rather obvious, it may not be essential to develop it to a second level. This is the completion of the top down development. More complex programs may go to a third and fourth or more levels before all logic is completed. Figure 6–4 shows the combined logic.

1. Print Headings

    1.1   Print Heading Line 1

    1.2   Print Heading Line 2

    1.3   Print Heading Line 3

2. Read Data

3. Calculate Costs

    3.1 Labor Cost is Hours times Labor Rate

    3.2 Overhead Cost is Hours times Overhead Rate

    3.3 Total Cost is Material Cost plus Labor Cost plus Overhead Cost

4. Print Detail

5. Print Total

6. Stop

Fig. 6-4

The concepts of top down logic will be further developed throughout this chapter as the need arises. Now we will examine some basic concepts of structured programming.

Structured Programming

The main thing to learn here is that a structured program is one which has a finite number of ways to write logic. By controlling the methods used, our programming will be more consistent, contain fewer errors, and be easier to read and debug. The methods used will be limited to three basic control structures.

Control Structure 1—Sequence

The first control structure is shown in Fig. 6-5. It represents a sequence of processing steps to be executed by the program in the order written. These steps

Fig. 6-5 *Sequence*

can be arithmetic operations, input/output commands, assignments, etc. A basic property of a control structure is that it has only one point at which it is entered and one point where it exits. Thus a sequence always begins at the first statement and ends at the last statement.

An example of a sequence control structure is given in Fig. 6-5.

Control Structure 2—If-Then-Else

Figure 6-6 shows the concept of an If-Then-Else control structure. Again there is only one entry and one exit point. The crucial part here is the decision (IF) which evaluates a condition and then chooses one of the actions. If the condition is true, the Then action is executed. However, if the condition is false,

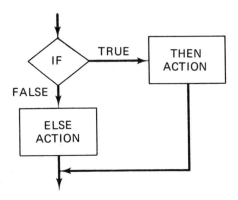

Fig. 6-6   *If-Then-Else*

the Else action will be executed. A Then action may, if necessary, be a Sequence Control Structure when a number of actions need to be taken. This also applies to the Else action. We will see later that the action may in fact be another If-Then-Else Control Structure.

An example of this control structure may be a simple choice between adding or subtracting an amount to/from a balance. This may be expressed as follows:

IF credit THEN subtract amount from balance
ELSE add amount to balance

The above expression states the condition and the actions to be taken if the condition is true and if it is false. It is not always necessary to have both true and false actions. Sometimes action is taken only when a condition is true. At other times, action is taken only when a condition is false. In these cases only the appropriate action needs to be specified.

Control Structure 3—Do While

The Do While Control Structure in Fig. 6-7 shows a single entry and exit structure which permits iteration of actions. The While is a decision which evaluates true or false in a manner similar to the IF. A true evaluation causes the

DO action to be executed. As long as (while) the condition evaluates true, the action will be repeated. When a false occurs, the sequence is completed and

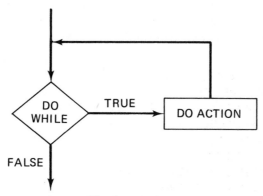

Fig. 6-7 *Do While*

control leaves by the exit. The action may consist of any other control structure as the need arises.

A simple example of the Do While is a case of reading cards, calculating an amount and printing.

1. Read initial card

2. Do While cards are available

    2.1 Amount is quantity times cost

    2.2 Print

    2.3 Read next card

3. Stop

The Do While consists of all step 2 statements. It indicates all statements at step 2 are to be executed until there are no more cards. When the supply of input cards is exhausted, step 3 stops the program. Notice that within the Do While, the statements are a sequence control structure.

Control Structures in PL/I

In Chapter 1 we looked at a sample program which read a payroll card, calculated the gross salary, and printed a line. The top down for this program is very simple.

1. Read a Payroll Card

2. Calculate Gross=(Hours∗Rate)−Tax

3. Print Payroll Data

This utilizes the sequence control structure. The PL/I program for this is shown in Fig. 6-8. Notice that in top down

```
1  PAY:PROC OPTIONS (MAIN);
2  DCL PAYNO FIXED(5),
       HOURS FIXED(2),
       RATE FIXED(4,2),
       TAX FIXED(5,2),
       GROSS FIXED(5,2);
3  GET LIST(PAYNO,HOURS,RATE,TAX);
4  GROSS=(HOURS∗RATE)−TAX;
5  PUT LIST(PAYNO,HOURS,RATE,GROSS);
6  END;
```

Fig. 6-8

development, certain things are understood to be present. The Procedure and End statements, being a part of every PL/I program, do not need to be referenced in the development of the logic. Declare statements are also understood to be needed in each program and therefore are not a part of the top down development.

The program in Fig. 6-8 is hardly realistic for the business environment. Most companies which use data processing systems have hundreds or even thousands of personnel on their payroll. And, of course, payroll itself is far more complex than the calculation of gross in the above program. However, for now we will concern ourselves with the handling of large quantities of data.

We want to rewrite the payroll program so that an unknown number of cards may be read and processed. That is, each card is read, gross is calculated and a line is printed. This process is repeated for every card in the input. Anything that is to be done repetitively uses the Do While control structure. Based on this we can then develop our top down logic.

1. Read a Card

2. Repeat processing until no cards

3. Stop

This level states in general terms our intentions. However, there is insufficient detail to write the program since step 2 needs to be refined.

2.   Repeat processing until no cards

    2.1 Calculate Gross=(Hours∗Rate)−Tax

    2.2 Print Payroll Data

    2.3 Read next Card

This level of development shows that these statements are to be repeated until no more cards are available. The first step in level 2 calculates the gross. Next, a detail line is printed. Then another card is read in preparation for repeating level 2 again. If we attempt to read the next card and there are no more cards, then the logic progresses to step 3 and the program terminates. This is why the Read occurs at the end of the Do While group.

To write this program in PL/I, the following combined top down development is used

1.   Read a Card

2.   Repeat processing until no cards

    2.1 Calculate Gross=(Hours∗Rate)−Tax

    2.2 Print Payroll Data

    2.3 Read next Card

3.   Stop

Since this logic uses the Do While control structure the next section discusses the PL/I DO WHILE statement.

Do While

The DO WHILE statement (Fig. 6-9) combined with an END statement permits a group of PL/I statements to be executed repetitively. An element-expression in the DO WHILE states the condition under which the Do group is to be executed. The group will execute as long as the expression is true. When the expression becomes false the program proceeds to the statement following the END.

```
1 2

DO WHILE (element-expression);
  •
  •
  •
END;
```

Fig. 6-9

DO   Keyword identifying the beginning of a DO group.

WHILE   Keyword indicating this is a DO WHILE group.

(*element-expression*)   Consists of at least two operands or expressions separated by a comparison operator (Fig. 6-10). The element-expression is evaluated to determine a true or false condition.

END;   Keyword indicating the end of the DO WHILE group. All statements to be executed in the group will be located between the DO and END statements.

=	Equal To
<	Less Than
>	Greater Than
<=	Less Than or Equal To
>=	Greater Than or Equal To
¬=	Not Equal To
¬<	Not Less Than
¬>	Not Greater Than
&	And
|	Or

Fig. 6-10 *Comparison Operators*

The DO WHILE may vary from quite simple expressions to very complex ones depending upon the need of the DO group. Some examples are:

DO WHILE(N=0);

This is a simple expression which causes the DO to execute the statement between the DO and the END until the value of N is no longer equal to zero.

DO WHILE(J>K);

This group executes until J becomes either less than K or equal to K. In each use of a DO WHILE, the expression is evaluated at the beginning. If the expression is already false, the Do group is not executed even the first time. Instead, control passes to the statement following the end. When the expression evaluates true, the entire Do group is executed before the expression is evaluated again. Therefore, if the expression becomes false part way through the Do group, the program continues to the END statement before another evaluation is made.

Some other examples of expressions are:

DO WHILE (K<= N+1);
DO WHILE (A=4 | B=N);
DO WHILE (J⌐= A*B);

When "and" appears with an "or" in an expression, the "and" is evaluated first. If this is not desired, brackets may be used to control priority.

DO WHILE (A=B&C>0|N=1);

If the "or" is to be evaluated first, write

DO WHILE (A=B&(C>0|N=1));

A Simple Payroll Program

Now we can write the program for payroll based on the top down development described earlier in the chapter. It is repeated here for easy reference.

1. Read a Card

2. Repeat processing until no cards

   2.1 Calculate Gross = (Hours * Rate)-Tax

   2.2 Print Payroll Data

   2.3 Read next card

3. Stop

The PL/I program for this logic is shown in Fig. 6-11 with some of the output. The program includes an ON ENDFILE statement which is not shown directly in the top down. This

```
01  PAY:PROC OPTIONS (MAIN);
02  DCL PAYNO FIXED(5),
        HOURS FIXED(2),
        RATE FIXED(4,2),
```

```
        TAX FIXED(5,2),
        GROSS FIXED(5,2);
03  DCL I FIXED(1) INIT(0);
04  ON ENDFILE(SYSIN) I=1;
06  GET LIST(PAYNO,HOURS,RATE,TAX);
07  DO WHILE(I=0);
08      GROSS=(HOURS*RATE)-TAX;
09      PUT SKIP LIST(PAYNO,HOURS,RATE,GROSS);
10      GET LIST(PAYNO,HOURS,RATE,TAX);
11      END;
12  END;
```

12345	35	4.50	127.50
23345	40	4.00	135.00
23350	35	5.00	140.00

Fig. 6-11

works with the DO WHILE to handle step 2 in the top down. To begin, the variable I is initialized to zero. This is tested in the DO WHILE. While I is equal to zero, the statements in the Do group (7-11) are repeated. When an attempt is made in statement 10 to get another card after the last has been read, the endfile statement sets I to one. Although the ON ENDFILE is in statement 4 it is effectively part of statement 10. Since the GET is the last statement in the Do group, the While condition is evaluated. I is not equal to zero so the Do terminates which in turn causes the program to terminate at statement 12.

IF,THEN,ELSE Statements

The IF statement (Fig. 6-12) permits the analysis of an element-expression and, depending upon the expression being true or false, selects the appropriate action to be taken. The element-expression is like that described in the DO WHILE. If the expression evaluates true, the THEN action is executed. If it evaluates false, the ELSE action is taken.

```
1 2

   IF element-expression THEN action-if-true;
                          ELSE action-if-false;
```

Fig. 6-12

IF	Keyword identifying a conditional statement.
element-expression	Consists of at least two operands or expressions separated by a comparison operator (Figure 6-10). The element-expression is evaluated to determine a true or false condition.
THEN	Keyword which is followed by the action to be taken if the element-expression is true. If THEN is followed immediately with a semicolon (THEN;), it is a null then indicating no action is necessary if the expression is true.
action-if-true;	May be any PL/I statement to be executed if the element-expression is true.
ELSE	Keyword which is followed by the action to be taken if the element-expression is false. It is optional and therefore may be absent when there is no false action. It could also be written as a null else.
action-if-false;	May be a PL/I statement to be executed if the element-expression is true.

The following statements show how the IF statement may be used.

1. If A=B then add 1 to Num.

2. Subtract 1 from Sum

```
IF A=B THEN NUM=NUM+1;
SUM = SUM-1;
```

If A is equal to B then the value 1 is added to NUM. Control then passes to the next statement and 1 is subtracted from SUM. If A was not equal to B the value in NUM is unchanged and 1 is subtracted from SUM.

1.1   If A=B then add 1 to NUM

1.2   else subtract 1 from SUM

```
IF A = B THEN NUM=NUM+1;
        ELSE SUM=SUM-1;
```

In this case 1 is added to NUM only if A equals B and SUM is unchanged. When A is not equal to B only SUM is affected by the operation.

1.1   If A=B and C=D then no action

1.2   · else amount=quantity∗value

```
IF A=B & C=D THEN;
             ELSE AMT=QTY∗VALUE;
```

This statement uses a compound condition. Both A=B and C=D must be true. If they are, no action is taken because of the null then. If the expression evaluates false, the value for AMT is computed in the else clause.

1.1   If name is Jones then Put salary

```
IF NAME = 'JONES' THEN PUT EDIT(SALARY)(F(6,2));
```

In this example a character string is tested for an alphabetic value. If the name contains the characters 'JONES' the Put statement is executed.

Nested IF

A nested IF statement is one which is contained in the action of another IF statement. Either the Then clause or the Else clause or both may contain another IF statement.

1.1   If name is Jones then

1.2   If salary>10000 then tax=35%

1.3   else tax=25%

```
IF NAME = 'JONES' THEN
       IF SALARY>10000 THEN TAX=0.35;
                         ELSE TAX=0.25;
```

The first condition to be met is the name must be Jones. If this is true the nested IF is then evaluated. If salary exceeds 10000, then 35% is assigned to TAX. If salary is less than or equal to 10000, then 25% is assigned to TAX. If the name was not Jones, the entire nested IF is bypassed.

Overdrawn Personal Accounts

The following program utilizes the IF statement to select from a set of data cards customers who have personal accounts in an overdrawn status. A personal account is a status code 3 and an overdraft is identified by a negative account balance. The report is to list all code 3 customers with a negative balance. The following card format is used.

1-6	Account Number	
7	Status Code	1 - Business
		2 - Checking
		3 - Personal
		4 - Credit
8-15	Customer Name	
16-21	Account Balance	

Based on this information we can develop the top down for the program as follows:

1.   Read Initial Card

2.   Repeat until no more cards

    2.1.1   If status = 3 then

    2.1.2   if balance <0 then print customer record

    2.2   Read next card

3.   Stop

The PL/I program for this top down is shown in Fig. 6–13. Steps 2.1.1 and 2.1.2 are shown as nested IF statements. This is the most direct way of identifying the two separate decisions. They could of course be combined in a compound if using the "and" symbol.

```
01   REPORT:PROC OPTIONS(MAIN);
02   DCL I FIXED(1) INIT(0),
        ACT FIXED(6),
        STATUS FIXED(1),
        NAME CHAR(8),
        BAL FIXED(6,2);
03   ON ENDFILE(SYSIN) I=1;
05   GET EDIT(ACT,STATUS, NAME, BAL) (R(CARD));
```

```
06  CARD:FORMAT(SKIP,F(6),F(1),A(8),F(6,2));
07  DO WHILE(I=0);
08     IF STATUS = 3 THEN
09        IF BAL <0 THEN
10           PUT EDIT(ACT,NAME,BAL) (F(6),X(2),A(8),X(2),F(7,2));
11     GET EDIT(ACT,STATUS,NAME,BAL) (R(CARD));
12     END;
13  END;
```

Fig. 6–13

An output from this program might be

> 235661   EMCO   –150.00

Do Statement

In the program in Fig. 6–13, only one action is taken in each THEN clause of the IF statements. Many times, more than one action needs to be taken if a condition is true. This may also be the case when the condition is false. A simple form of the DO statement allows any number of actions to be associated with the THEN clause and the ELSE clause. The basic form of this statement is

---

IF *element-expression* THEN DO;
        actions-if-true
        END;
        ELSE DO;
        actions-if-false
        END;

The actions may consist of any valid PL/I statements including another IF statement. Each DO requires a matching END to show the scope of the Do.

IF N = 1 THEN DO;
    K = K + J;
    PUT LIST(K);
    END;

In this example, if the value of N is equal to 1, then the two statements between the DO and END are executed and control continues at the statement following the END. If N is not equal to 1, control passes immediately to the statement following the END.

```
IF A = B THEN DO;
       NUM = NUM + 1;
       TOTAL = TOTAL + VALUE;
       PROD = A * * 2;
       END;
       ELSE DO;
       NUM = NUM-1;
       PROD = A * B;
       END;
```

If A equals B, the three expressions in the THEN DO group are executed and the ELSE DO group is bypassed. When A is not equal to B, only the ELSE DO group is executed. In either case control continues after the final end.

A DO group with a nested IF,THEN,DO is shown in the next example.

```
IF A=B  THEN DO;
        NUM = NUM +1;
        IF C = D THEN DO;
               TOTAL = TOTAL + VALUE;
               R = K * T;
               END;
               ELSE DO;
               S = K + R;
               PUT LIST (S);
               END;
        ELSE PUT LIST (NUM);
```

This program doesn't do anything in particular but simply shows how nesting can be used with DO groups. When A equals B, the value 1 is added to NUM and the nested IF is evaluated. If C = D, then the inner set of expressions are computed. Value is added to total and K is multiplied by T. If C was not equal to D, the inner ELSE DO is executed. Whether C = D or not, the value of A must still equal B since we are still inside the A = B DO group. If A does not equal B, control passes immediately to the last ELSE statement and the value of NUM is printed.

Page Overflow

The program in Figure 6-13 produced only 1 line of output since only one data record met all of the requirements. However, in a more realistic situation there may be hundreds of records which meet the necessary requirements. In this case we would get many pages of output. On each page we should have a heading to identify the printed values. There may also be a need for a total of all overdrawn balances to be printed at the end of the report. The top down for this problem is as follows:

   1.   Read Initial Card

   2.   Repeat until no more cards

          2.1   IF page overflow print headings

          2.2.1 IF status = 3 then

          2.2.2   IF balance <0 then

          2.2.3   process customer record

          2.3   Read next card

   3.   Print total

   4.   Stop

Further development is needed to show how 2.1, the page overflow, and 2.2.3, process customer records, are handled. This development follows.

     2.1.1   IF line = 30 then do

     2.1.2   Set line to 0

     2.1.3   Print heading lines 1, 2 and 3

     2.1.4   Skip a line

     2.2.3.1 Print Detail line

     2.2.3.2 Add balance to total

     2.2.3.3 Add 1 to line

Initially the line counter has been set to 30 to indicate 30 detail lines per page. This number will depend upon the printer layout and length of paper used. For testing purposes it is sometimes useful to set the number to a low value, like 5, so that smaller amounts of data may be used to test for page overflow. The combined top down is now shown.

   1.   Read Initial Card

   2.   Repeat until no more cards

   2.1.1   If line = 30 then

   2.1.2   Set line to 0

2.1.3   Print heading lines 1, 2 and 3

2.1.4   Skip a line

2.2.1   IF status = 3 then

2.2.2   IF balance <0 then

2.2.3.1   Print Detail line

2.2.3.2   Add balance to total

2.2.3.3   Add 1 to line

2.3   Read next card

3.   Print total

4.   Stop

This program is written in Fig. 6-14 showing some output and a total line. Notice that the heading for the first page is produced by initializing LINE to 30 in the declare. This forces an overflow before the first record is processed and a heading is printed.

```
1   REPORT:PROC OPTIONS(MAIN);
2   DCL I FIXED(1) INIT(0),
         ACT FIXED(6),
         STATUS FIXED(1),
         NAME CHAR(8),
         BAL FIXED(6,2);
3   DCL TOTAL FIXED(7,2) INIT(0),
         LINE FIXED(2) INIT(30);
4   ON ENDFILE(SYSIN) I=1;
6   GET EDIT(ACT,STATUS,NAME,BAL) (R(CARD));
7   CARD:FORMAT(SKIP,F(6),F(1),A(8),F(6,2));
8   DO WHILE(I=0);
9      IF LINE = 30 THEN DO;
11        LINE = 0;
12        PUT EDIT('OVERDRAWN ACCOUNTS') (PAGE,X(7),A);
13        PUT EDIT('ACCOUNT      NAME        BALANCE') (SKIP(2),A);
14        PUT EDIT('NUMBER') (SKIP,A);
15        PUT SKIP;
16        END;
17     IF STATUS = 3 THEN
18        IF BAL <0 THEN DO;
20           PUT EDIT(ACT,NAME,BAL)(SKIP,F(6),X(6),A(8),X(5),F(7,2));
```

```
21          TOTAL=TOTAL-BAL;
22          LINE=LINE+1;
23          END;
24      GET EDIT(ACT,STATUS,NAME,BAL) (R(CARD));
25      END;
26  PUT EDIT('TOTAL OVERDRAWN',TOTAL)(SKIP(2),X(7),A,X(2),F(8,2));
27  END;
```

OVERDRAWN ACCOUNTS		
ACCOUNT NUMBER	NAME	BALANCE
123655	NELSON	-25.00
235000	JACKSON	-255.79
236550	KENT	-6.75
TOTAL OVERDRAWN		287.54

Fig. 6-14   *Reports with Page Overflow*

When the total is accumulated, a minus is used. This is necessary since the values being accumulated are negative numbers. Using a minus gives a positive total.

Iterative DO

In the preceding DO groups, the statements within the group were executed once after which control left the group. The iterative DO permits the statements to be executed over and over again (iteratively) until a given condition is reached. The DO statement itself controls the number of iterations. The general format for iterative DO is shown in Fig. 6-15.

```
DO variable = specification 1 TO specification 2
                  BY specification 3;
        .
        .
        .
     END;
```

Fig. 6-15

DO	Keyword specifying the beginning of the DO group.
variable	A variable which is used to count the number of iterations.
=*specification* 1	A constant, variable name, or expression which represents the initial or beginning value of the variable.
TO *specification* 2	A constant, variable name, or expression which represents the terminal value of variable.
BY *specification* 3	Optional—constant, variable name or expression by which the variable is incremented after each iteration of the DO group. If omitted the value 1 is assumed.

Sum of 1 To 10

Figure 6-16 demonstrates the use of a simple DO to find the sum of all integers from 1 to 10 inclusive.

```
01   SUM1:PROC OPTIONS(MAIN);
02   DCL SUM FIXED(5) INIT(0);
03   DO I=1 TO 10;
04       SUM=SUM+I;
05       END;
06   PUT EDIT('THE SUM OF 1 TO 10 IS',SUM) (A,X(1),F(5));
07   END;
```

```
THE SUM OF 1 TO 10 IS     55
```

Fig. 6-16

In this program I begins with the value 1. Within the DO, the value of I is added to SUM. At the END, the value of I is increased by 1 and the loop executes a second time. This time 2 is added to SUM. This process continues until I becomes 10. At this point the loop is finished and execution continues at the PUT EDIT.

Sum of any Set of Values

This program sums 1 to 10 very nicely but for any other values the program would need to be changed. To improve this a second program has been written (Fig. 6-17) which allows for any starting value (START), any increment (INC), and any terminating value (LAST). These values are provided on a data card. The program allows any number of sums to be computed by providing a data card for each set of values. Since any set of values may be provided, we must guard against a range which would cause the SUM to overflow. This is accomplished by calculating the difference between START and LAST. If this exceeds 1000, a message is printed and the sum is not calculated.

```
 1  SUM2:PROC OPTIONS(MAIN);
 2  DCL SUM FIXED(8) INIT(0),
        (START,INC,LAST) FIXED(5),
        N FIXED(1) INIT(0);
 3  ON ENDFILE(SYSIN) N=1;
 5  GET EDIT(START,INC,LAST)(3 F(5));
 6  DO WHILE (N=0);
 7     IF LAST−START > 1000 THEN
 8        PUT EDIT('RANGE EXCEEDS 1000') (SKIP,A);
 9        ELSE DO;
10           DO I=START TO LAST BY INC;
11              SUM=SUM+I;
12              END;
13           PUT EDIT('THE SUM OF',START,' TO',LAST,' BY',INC,' IS',
                 SUM) (SKIP,3 (A,F(6)),A,F(8));
14           SUM=0;
15           END;
16     GET EDIT(START,INC,LAST) (SKIP,3 F(5));
17     END;
18  END;
```

```
THE SUM OF          1 TO    100 BY    1 IS    5050
THE SUM OF        100 TO   1000 BY   10 IS   50050
RANGE EXCEEDS    1000
```

Fig. 6-17

Temperature Conversion Charts

The iterative Do is also useful in programs that generate charts. Suppose we want a list of equivalent Fahrenheit temperatures for 1 to 30 degrees Celsius (centigrade). The formula is

$$F = \frac{5}{9}C + 32$$

The purpose of the Do loop in this program (Fig. 6-18) is to generate the values for Celsius (CEL). Within the DO, the formula is used to calculate the equivalent degree in Fahrenheit (FAH). Then the two values (CEL and FAH) are printed. The Do ends and the next value for CEL is determined. This process continues until 30 is reached.

```
01  CELSIUS:PROC OPTIONS(MAIN);
02  DCL (CEL,FAH) FIXED(2);
03  PUT EDIT('CELSIUS FAHRENHEIT')(A);
04  PUT SKIP;
05  DO CEL= 1 TO 30;
06      FAH=(CEL*9)/5+32;
07      PUT EDIT(CEL,FAH) (SKIP,X(3),F(2),X(7),F(2));
08      END;
09  END;
```

CELSIUS	FAHRENHEIT
1	33
2	35
3	37
4	39
5	41
6	42
7	44
8	46
9	48
10	50
11	51
12	53
13	55
14	57
15	59
16	60
17	62
18	64
19	66
20	68
21	69
22	71
23	73
24	75
25	77
26	78

27	80
28	82
29	84
30	86

Fig. 6-18

One problem with the approach taken in Fig. 6-18 is that a long column of figures is produced. If many more degrees Celsius were desired several pages of output may be generated. This would make use of the table rather awkward. A more appropriate output would be a chart. The program is rewritten in Fig. 6-19 to produce a chart or matrix of values.

```
01  CELSIUS:PROC OPTIONS (MAIN);
02  DCL (CEL,FAH) FIXED(3);
03  DO I=1 TO 5;
04     PUT EDIT('C','F') (X(5),A,X(3),A);
05     END;
06  PUT SKIP(2);
07  DO I=1 TO 26 BY 5;
08     DO CEL=I TO I+4;
09        FAH=(CEL*9)/5+32;
10        PUT EDIT(CEL,FAH) (X(4),F(2),X(2),F(2));
11        END;
12     PUT SKIP;
13     END;
14  END;
```

C	F	C	F	C	F	C	F	C	F
1	33	2	35	3	37	4	39	5	41
6	42	7	44	8	46	9	48	10	50
11	51	12	53	13	55	14	57	15	59
16	60	17	62	18	64	19	66	20	68
21	69	22	71	23	73	24	75	25	77
26	78	27	80	28	82	29	84	30	86

Fig. 6-19

First a heading is necessary. This is accomplished using a DO loop instead of repeating the characters F and C in the Put Edit. Since no SKIP is used in the format list the characters continue to print on the same line.

Next we want to generate the chart. Here it is necessary to visualize the output we desire to establish the beginning value for each line (1,6,11,etc.).

Based on this we can write the first DO which generates these starting values in I. However this does not produce the Celsius temperature for each line. For this a nested DO is used. This DO generates values beginning at I and ending at I+4 for every line.

Within the nested DO, the value for FAH is computed. Both CEL and FAH are printed without using SKIP. This inner loop causes 5 pairs of values to be printed. When the loop ends a PUT SKIP is executed which will cause the next repetition of the Do loop to begin printing on the following print line.

Variations of the Do

The following examples show additional ways in which Do statements may be written. The first shows the use of negative values.

```
DO I = 10 TO 1 BY -1;
DO N = J TO -K BY -L;
```

Expressions may also be used in any of the specifications of the Do statement.

```
DO K = N*2 TO J+L BY 2;
DO N = 1 TO I* *2;
```

In the case of an expression, the value of the specification is determined through an arithmetic calculation. The starting value of K above is determined by multiplying N by 2. If N was the value 5, the starting value in K would be 10.

Fractional values may also be used as follows.

```
DO A = .5 TO 5.0 BY .5;
DO B = C TO D BY .01;
```

In these Do statements, care must be exercised in the choice of variable names. Default names are not advised but rather each name used should be declared with appropriate fractional precision.

The While clause discussed earlier may also be combined with an iterative Do.

```
DO I = 1 TO 100 WHILE (N=K);
```

When this statement is encountered, the Do will iterate normally while N=K. If N and K remain equal, processing will continue until I=100. However, if prior to this time N becomes unequal to K, the iteration process will terminate and control will pass out of the Do loop.

Another form of the Do allows for a multiple range to be specified.

DO I = 1 TO 10, 15 TO 20, 33 TO 39 BY 3;

In this case, I varies from 1 to 10 using increments of 1. When 10 is reached, I is set to 15 and is varied to 20 by 1. Finally I is set to 33 and increased by 3 until 39 is reached. At this point the iteration is terminated.

DO K = 3, 5, 7, 14, 29;

This Do sets K to specific values. Only the values entered above are assigned to K in the order specified. In this case only 5 iterations of the loop are necessary, once for each of the values in the Do statement.

STOP Statement

When control in a program reaches the Procedure END statement, the program is automatically terminated. Sometimes it is convenient to terminate a program without going to the END statement. This can be done with a STOP statement. The general format is

---

STOP;

Sequence Checking

To demonstrate the STOP we will use the report program from Figure 6-14. This program has been reproduced in Figure 6-20 with the addition of a sequence check. The purpose

```
01   REPORT:PROC OPTIONS(MAIN);
02   DCL I FIXED(1) INIT(0),
         ACT FIXED(6),
         STATUS FIXED(1),
         NAME CHAR(8),
         BAL FIXED(6,2);
03   DCL TOTAL FIXED(7,2) INIT(0),
         LINE FIXED(2) INIT(30);
04   DCL PREV FIXED(6) INIT(0);
05   ON ENDFILE(SYSIN) I=1;
06   GET EDIT(ACT,STATUS,NAME,BAL) (R(CARD));
```

```
07  CARD:FORMAT(SKIP,F(6),F(1),A(8),F(6,2));
08  DO WHILE(I=0);
09      IF ACT <= PREV THEN DO;
10          PUT EDIT('SEQUENCE ERROR IN ACCOUNT',ACT)
                        (SKIP,A,X(2),F(6));
11          STOP;
12          END;
13      PREV=ACT;
14      IF LINE = 30 THEN DO;
15          LINE = 0;
16          PUT EDIT('OVERDRAWN ACCOUNTS') (PAGE,X(7),A);
17          PUT EDIT('ACCOUNT      NAME      BALANCE') (SKIP(2),A);
18          PUT EDIT('NUMBER') (SKIP,A);
19          PUT SKIP;
20          END;
21      IF STATUS = 3 THEN
              IF BAL <0 THEN DO;
22              PUT EDIT(ACT,NAME,BAL) (SKIP,F(6),X(6),A(8),X(5),F(7,2));
23              TOTAL=TOTAL-BAL;
24              LINE=LINE+1;
25              END;
26      GET EDIT(ACT,STATUS,NAME,BAL) (R(CARD));
27      END;
28  PUT EDIT ('TOTAL OVERDRAWN',TOTAL)(SKIP(2),X(7),A,X(2),F(8,
    2));
29  END;
```

Fig. 6-20

of a sequence check is to ensure that data is read in a specified order. In this case we want the cards to be in account number sequence, beginning with the lowest account number and proceeding to the highest. The statements used to check for sequence on each card are:

```
IF ACT<= PREV THEN DO;
    PUT EDIT ('SEQUENCE ERROR IN ACCOUNT',ACT)
            (SKIP, A,X(2),F(6));
    STOP;
    END;
PREV=ACT;
```

As each card is read, its account number is compared to the account number in PREV. When the first card is read there is no previous account so PREV contains zero. Therefore the first account will be greater than zero. The account number of this card is then moved to previous. When the next card is read, its account will be compared to the account from the previous card. If this account is less than or equal to the previous an error message is printed and the program is stopped.

Programming Problems

1. Modify the results of Programming Problems 1 and 2 from Chapter 5 to read *n* data cards.

2. Modify the results of Problem 4 from Chapter 5 to read cards for *n* salesmen. Compute totals for total sales amount, total gross, and total net. These are to be printed at the end of the report. Provide sufficient data so that more than one page of printout is produced. Each page must have headings preceding the data.

3. A company requires a payroll report which lists the earnings for each employee in each department. There is one card per employee. Cards are in employee within department number sequence. Each card should be checked for sequence on both fields and the program stopped if a sequence error occurs.

    One line of output is needed for each card showing all input data as well as tax amount, gross salary, total deductions and net salary. At the end of each department, print totals for hours, tax amount, savings, union, pension, gross, total deductions, and net. At the end of the report show these totals again for all departments.

Col.	1-5	Employee Number
	6-8	Department Number
	9-11	Hours Worked
	12-15	Hourly Rate
	16-18	Tax Percentage
	19-22	Savings Deduction
	23-26	Union Deduction
	27-30	Pension Deduction

4. Using the cards from Problem 3, produce a departmental summary report showing only the totals for each department and overall totals for all departments. Do not print a detail line for each card.

5. A computer dating service wishes to produce a listing of all single females between 19 and 21 inclusive who have blue eyes and blond hair. Examine the codes in the following data cards to produce this report. (*Option:* list all single males with these characteristics.)

Col.	1-2	Age	
	3	Sex	1 – Male
			2 – Female
	4	Marital Status	1 – Single
			2 – Married
			3 – Divorced
			4 – Separated
	5	Eye Color	1 – Brown
			2 – Green
			3 – Blue
	6	Hair Color	1 – Blond
			2 – Brunette
			3 – Red
	7-30	Name	
	31-70	Address	
	71-80	Phone Number (Including Area Code)	

6. Using the data cards of Problem 5, count the number of males and females in each marital status. This produces eight totals. Print these totals, indicating the percentage each of them represent of the entire data deck.

7. In the current year the population of Toronto is 2 million and the population of Hamilton is 250,000. Assume that Toronto grows at a constant rate of 2 percent per year and Hamilton grows at 5 percent per year. In what year will they have an equal population?

8. A student who leaves school at 21 plans to save $40.00 per month until retiring at age 65. Given a constant interest rate of 9 percent per year, computed monthly, what will this investment amount to upon retirement?

9. Write a program to produce a table of equivalent temperatures in Celsius for temperatures in Fahrenheit from 1 to 120 degrees. The formula for conversion from Fahrenheit to Celsius is $C = (F - 32) \times 5/9$.

10. Write a program to find all three digit numbers whose value is equal to the sum of the cube of the digits.

11. Write a program to produce a chart which is useful for converting gallons used and miles driven into miles per gallon. Depending on the range of values you choose, several pages of output may be required.

12. There are 2.54 centimeters per inch. Produce a table showing the equivalent centimeters for lengths from 1 inch to 8 feet. Show these lengths in feet and inches in your table.

13. Compound interest may be calculated using the formula $S = P(1 + i)^n$ where S = compound interest, P = principal, i = interest rate per period, n = num-

ber of periods. Write a program to compute the value of an investment of $8000 at 8½% compounded annually for a period of 5 years. Compare the results using an iterative technique.

14. Rewrite problem 13 by compounding the interest quarterly. Compare the results.

7

Arrays and
Subscripted Variables

Many programming applications involve repetitive data items such as lists and tables. Even though each data item in the group could be declared individually, this is an inefficient and awkward approach. For example, a group of student cards might each be organized as follows:

COLUMNS	DATA
1–9	Student Number
10–24	Name
26–28	Mark obtained in subject 1
29–31	Mark obtained in subject 2
32–34	Mark obtained in subject 3
35–37	Mark obtained in subject 4
38–40	Mark obtained in subject 5
41–43	Mark obtained in subject 6

To read this data and compute each student's average mark requires the declaration of 8 variables for the data card plus one for the average itself. However, each mark is similar in type and length. The difference lies in the actual data itself.

One-Dimensional Arrays

Repetitive data of this type may be declared as a one-dimensional array. The general format for an array declaration is shown in Fig. 7-1.

---

1 | 2

DECLARE *identifier* (*dimension*) *base scale* (*precision*);

Fig. 7-1

DECLARE	
identifier	See Chapter 3 for an explanation of these
base	attributes
scale	
(*precision*)	
(*dimension*)	An unsigned integer number for a single dimension array, e.g., (10) specifies a one-dimensional array with 10 elements.
	(3,5) specifies a two-dimensional array with a total of 15 (3×5) elements.

Applying this to the student card, the declare would be as follows:

```
DCL NUM FIXED(9),NAME CHAR(15),
    MARK(6) FIXED(3);
DCL TØT FIXED(3), AVG FIXED(3,1);
```

MARK is a one-dimension array comprised of 6 elements each capable of storing a 3-digit FIXED DECIMAL number. Thus all six of the MARKs from the data card may be stored in this array. The following GET statement will read the data card into the above variables.

```
GET EDIT(NUM,NAME,MARK)(F(9),A(15),6 F(3));
```

Since MARK is a 6-element array the format item 6 F(3) causes six variables to be transferred from the data record to the array.

If the data had been

710235018KR RØSLYN 073081065078085068

the contents of the array after the GET would appear as follows:

MARK	73	81	65	78	85	68
	(1)	(2)	(3)	(4)	(5)	(6)

Each MARK within the array may be referred to individually by using a subscript with the array name.

```
1 2

  identifier (subscript)
```

In this program the *identifier* is MARK. If we wish to refer to the first MARK within the array, the expression MARK(1) is used. MARK(3) refers to the third MARK and MARK(6) to the sixth MARK.

A subscript must be an integer constant or variable and is not permitted to exceed the bounds of the declared array. Thus only values from 1 to 6 inclusive would be valid subscripts for MARK.

When a variable is used, the present value of the variable becomes the subscript.

```
01   I = 5;

02   K = MARK(I);
```

Since I contains the value 5, the effective result of statement 02 is

$$K = MARK(5);$$

Thus the fifth element of MARK is assigned to K.

Using a variable subscript, the total of the MARKs may be developed in TØT and AVG calculated as follows:

```
TØT = 0;
DØ I = 1 TØ 6;
TØT = TØT+MARK(I);
END;
AVG = TØT/6;
```

The DØ loop is repeated 6 times with I assuming values 1 to 6. Thus each element of MARK is added into TØT. When all six MARKs have been summed, TØT is divided by 6 giving AVG.

The procedure in Fig. 7-2 combines these statements into a program which has an indefinite number of student cards, computes each student's average, and prints all of the input data with this average.

```
 1  AVER:PROC OPTIONS(MAIN);
 2  DCL NUM FIXED(9),
        NAME CHAR(15),
        MARK(6) FIXED(3),
        TOT FIXED(3),
        AVG FIXED(3,1);
 3  ON ENDFILE(SYSIN) STOP;
 5  PUT EDIT('NUMBER','NAME','MARKS','AVERAGE')
            (PAGE,A,COL(17),A,COL(39),A,COL(55),A);
 6  PUT SKIP(2);
 7  DO WHILE('1'B);
 8      GET EDIT (NUM,NAME,MARK) (COL(1),F(9),A(15),6 F(3));
 9      TOT=0;
10      DO I=1 TO 6;
11          TOT=TOT+MARK(I);
12          END;
13      AVG=TOT/6;
14      PUT EDIT(NUM,NAME,MARK,AVG)
            (SKIP,F(9),X(2),A(15),X(2),6 F(4),X(4),F(4,1));
15      END;
16  END AVER;
```

NUMBER	NAME	MARKS						AVERAGE
459143462	JOHN SMITH	75	89	68	76	83	70	76.8
675867935	EDWARD MARTIN	70	45	63	59	55	63	59.1
756482745	KATHY DELRAY	78	63	80	76	88	84	78.1

Fig. 7-2

Finding the Highest Profit

In this problem we want to read a number of Product cards (maximum of 20). Each card contains the following information:

1-5 Product Number
6-20 Description
21-27 Profit Margin

To solve this problem we will use one dimension arrays to first store the data from the cards. Then the array containing the profit margin is searched to find the highest profit. This product is then printed with the related data.

The program for this solution is shown in Fig. 7-3 followed by some input data and the program output. Three separate arrays are used to store the card data. Each one has different attributes because of the nature of the data. Statements 5 to 7 load the data cards. K is used to determine when all cards have been read and terminates the loop. At this point I is reduced by 2 to compensate for the value in it when the loop is terminated.

Statements 9 to 17 find the product with the highest profit. This is done by first setting a variable HIGH to the value in the first element of MARGIN. L is set to 1 to indicate where this value was found. The DØ loop causes the remaining values of MARGIN to be referenced using the subscript N. Each of these values is compared to HIGH in statement 12. If any one is greater than HIGH, it is then stored in HIGH and its location, determined by subscript N, is stored in L.

When the loop is finished the data with the highest profit is printed.

```
1  PROD:PROC OPTIONS(MAIN);
2  DCL PRODUCT(20) FIXED(5),
       DESC(20) CHAR(15),
       MARGIN(20) FIXED(7,2),
       HIGH FIXED(7,2),
       K FIXED(1) INIT(0);
3  ON ENDFILE(SYSIN) K=1;
   /***** LOAD ARRAY *****/
5  DO I= 1 TO 20 WHILE(K=0);
6     GET EDIT(PRODUCT(I),DESC(I),MARGIN(I))
              (COL(1),F(5),A(15),F(7,2));
7     END;
8  I=I-2;
   /***** FIND PRODUCT WITH THE HIGHEST PROFIT MARGIN *****/
9  HIGH=MARGIN(1);
10 L=1;            /** L = LOCATION OF PRODUCT **/
11 DO N= 2 TO I;
12    IF MARGIN(N) > HIGH THEN DO;
14       HIGH = MARGIN(N);
15       L=N;
16       END;
```

```
17    END;
18  PUT EDIT('PRODUCT WITH HIGHEST PROFIT MARGIN')
          (PAGE,A)
              ('PRODUCT       DESCRIPTION       MARGIN')
          (SKIP(2),A)
          (PRODUCT(L),DESC(L),MARGIN(L))
          (SKIP(2),F(6),X(3),A(15),F(10,2));
19  END PROD;
```

Fig. 7-3

The program was run using the following input data:

```
12500WATER PUMP         0001275
12750REFRIGERATOR       0007825
13610MICROWAVE OVEN     0008600
13798HEATER             0003715
```

After processing the output produced was as follows:

```
PRODUCT WITH HIGHEST PROFIT MARGIN
PRODUCT      DESCRIPTION      MARGIN
 13610      MICROWAVE OVEN     86.00
```

A question at this point might be: What happens if there are two products with the same profit? The answer is that the first one encountered in the array will be the one to print. An interesting revision to the program would be to detect more than one product with the same highest profit and print both of them. This problem is left for the student to solve.

Initializing Arrays

In the chapter on declare statements we looked at the method for initializing variables. A similar approach may be used with arrays. The basic difference with an array is that each element may have a different value. For instance, the array NUM may contain 5 elements. To assign the values 10 17 19 20 25 to this array the following statement is used:

```
DCL NUM(5) FIXED(2) INIT(10,17,19,20,25);
```

Each value in the initial attribute is separated from the other with a comma. The position of each corresponds with the first through fifth position in the array.

All elements of an array may be assigned the same value using an iteration factor.

DCL SUM(100) FIXED(5) INIT((100)0);

Here the value 100 is an iteration factor which assigns the value zero to each of the 100 elements of SUM.

When character strings are involved, a repetition factor as well as the iteration factor is used. The repetition factor tells how many occurrences there are in the string. The iteration factor specifies the number of elements in the array.

DCL NAME (10) CHAR(15) INIT((10)(15)' ');

In this example 10 is the iteration factor indicating 10 elements of the array are affected by this initial attribute. The second entry 15 says each of the 15 bytes of an element is to receive a blank character.

Arrays As Tables

In this section arrays will be used as tables to look up information required for processing. In simple cases this information could be determined through a series of IF statements. This method becomes rather lengthy and awkward when a large number of decisions are necessary. In the following problem even as few as five discount percentages may be applied more effectively with a table than with a series of IFs.

The input data is in the following format:

1-5	Customer Number
6	Class
7 - 10	Item Number
11 - 14	Quantity
15 - 19	Unit Cost

The program is required to apply a discount to each customer based on the Class code in column 6. The customer is to pay an amount derived by multiplying the unit cost by the quantity and reducing the result by the discount. Discounts are 2, 3, 5, 7, and 10 percent for classes 1 through 5 respectively. A report is to be printed showing Customer Number, Item, Gross, Discount, and Net amounts.

Figure 7-4 shows the program with its resulting output. First notice how TABLE is initialized in statement 4. Each value is entered in the initial attribute in the order it appears in the array. Additional comments are placed in the program at this point as a reminder to the programmer of what the array values represent.

The main point of this program is how to use the array as a discount depending on the value found in Class. This is found in statement 12. At this point Gross has already been calculated (statement 11). Now the discount percent is found by using Class as a subscript for Table. If Class is 1 then the

```
 1  DISC:PROC OPTIONS(MAIN);
 2  DCL CUST FIXED(5),
        CLASS FIXED(1),
        ITEM CHAR(4),
        QTY FIXED(4),
        UNIT FIXED(5,2);
 3  DCL GROSS FIXED(6,2),
        DISCOUNT FIXED(5,2),
        NET FIXED(6,2);
 4  DCL TABLE(5) FIXED(2,2) INIT(.02,.03,.05,.07,.10);
        /*  CLASS   DISCOUNT  */
        /*    1        2%     */
        /*    2        3%     */
        /*    3        5%     */
        /*    4        7%     */
        /*    5       10%     */
 5  ON ENDFILE(SYSIN) STOP;
 7  PUT EDIT ('CUSTOMER    ITEM    GROSS DISCOUNT    NET')
                (PAGE, A);
 8  PUT SKIP(2);
 9  DO WHILE('1'B);
10      GET EDIT(CUST,CLASS,ITEM,QTY,UNIT)
                (COL(1),F(5),F(1),A(4),F(4),F(5,2));
11      GROSS=QTY*UNIT;
12      DISCOUNT=GROSS*TABLE(CLASS);
                        /* CLASS IS A SUBSCRIPT */
                        /* TO FIND DISCOUNT     */
                        /* PERCENT IN TABLE     */
13      NET=GROSS-DISCOUNT;
14      PUT EDIT(CUST,ITEM,GROSS,DISCOUNT,NET)
                (SKIP,F(6),X(5),A(4),X(3),F(7,2),F(8,2),F(10,2));
15      END;
16  END DISC;
```

CUSTOMER	ITEM	GROSS	DISCOUNT	NET
12300	A123	120.00	2.40	117.60
12500	C205	937.50	28.12	909.38
12750	X008	400.00	28.00	372.00
13610	A368	250.00	12.50	237.50
13789	L404	125.00	12.50	112.50

Fig. 7-4

subscript causes the first element of the table to be referenced and .02 is used as the discount. For instance, Customer Number 13610 had a Class of 3 in the data card. This caused the third element .05 to be used. The discount of 12.50 is 5% of 250.00. In the last data record the discount class was 5 and so .10 was selected.

Paired Tables

In the previous problem the solution was quite simple since the class code corresponded directly with each entry in the table. Unfortunately there are many cases when this is not so convenient. The following program reads cards containing a Salesman Number, Sales Amount, and a Basic Salary. Each salesman receives a commission in addition to the Basic Salary. The commission is based on sales according to the following table.

SALES	COMMISSION
00000-11999	5%
12000-13499	7%
13500-14999	10%
15000-19999	12%
20000 over	15%

The program in Fig. 7-5 shows how to implement a table like this in PL/I. Two arrays are needed, one for sales and the other for the commission percentages. Notice that the array

```
1  SALE:PROC OPTIONS(MAIN);
2  DCL NUM FIXED(5),
        AMOUNT FIXED(5),
```

```
        BASIC FIXED(6,2),
        COMMISSION FIXED(6,2);
 3  DCL GROSS FIXED(7,2),
        N FIXED(1) INIT(0),
        TOTCOM FIXED(7,2) INIT(0),
        TOTGROSS FIXED(8,2) INIT(0);
 4  DCL SALES(5) FIXED(5) INIT(11999,13499,14999,19999,99999),
        COM (5) FIXED(2,2) INIT(.05,.07,.10,.12,.15);
 5     ON ENDFILE(SYSIN) N=1;
 7     PUT EDIT('SALESMAN SALARY COMMISSION GROSS') (PAGE,A);
 8     PUT SKIP;
 9     GET EDIT(NUM,AMOUNT,BASIC) (COL(1),2 F(5),F(6,2));
10     DO WHILE(N=0);
11        DO I=1 TO 5;    /*SEARCH TABLE FOR SALES CATEGORY*/
12           IF AMOUNT < = SALES (I) THEN DO; /* FOUND          */
14              COMMISSION=AMOUNT*COM(I);
15              GROSS=BASIC+COMMISSION;
16              TOTCOM=TOTCOM+COMMISSION;
17              TOTGROSS=TOTGROSS+GROSS;
18              PUT EDIT(NUM,BASIC,COMMISSION,GROSS)
                        (SKIP,F(6),COL(11),F(7,2),COL(22),F(7,2),
                         COL(32),F(8,2));
19              I= 5     /*FORCES THE DO LOOP TO END */
20              END;
21           END;
22        GET EDIT(NUM,AMOUNT,BASIC) (COL(1),2 F(5),F(6,2));
23        END;
24     PUT EDIT('TOTALS',TOTCOM,TOTGROSS)
              (SKIP(2),COL(10),A,COL(21),F(8,2),COL(32),F(8,2));
25     END SALE;
```

Fig. 7-5

SALES contains only the high values for each sales category. Corresponding with each element of SALES is the percentage in each element of COM. There is a one to one relationship between these two arrays.

When a card is read, the array is searched for the correct sales category. This is done beginning at statement 11. The variable I is used as a subscript in statement 12 to compare the sales amount from the data card with the entry in the SALES table. When the AMOUNT is less than or equal to the table, the proper position is reached and I gives the location of the corresponding commission percentage to be used. This calculation is done in statement 14. Additional calculations are done in this inner DO group and a detail line is printed.

In statement 19, I is set to 5. This forces the DO loop to end regardless of where the search stopped. If the loop was not terminated each subsequent iteration would cause the inner Do to execute. This would produce invalid output.

Two-Dimensional Arrays

Data which is stored in a table or matrix form involves an array comprised of two dimensions. For example the PL/I declare statement

DCL TABLE(3,5) FIXED(2);

reserves 15 storage positions each capable of recording a two-digit number. This might be represented pictorially as follows:

COLUMN

	1	2	3	4	5
1					
ROW 2					
3					

The first dimension (3) in the DECLARE refers to the number of rows in the array. The second dimension (5) refers to the number of columns. Thus each element of the array may be referred to uniquely by the use of two subscripts.

TABLE (1,1) refers to the element which is at the intersection of row 1 and column 1, whereas TABLE (3,4) refers to the intersection of row 3 and column 4.

Internally the data in the computer is not actually stored in table form but, rather, in a linear fashion. Thus all data for one row is stored first, followed by the next row, etc. Figure 7–6 shows this organization.

TABLE

1,1	
1,2	
1,3	
1,4	
1,5	
2,1	
2,2	
2,3	
2,4	
2,5	
3,1	
3,2	
3,3	
3,4	
3,5	

Fig. 7–6

Two-dimensional arrays may be referred to using variable subscripts similar to one-dimensional arrays. In this case two different variables are required, one for each dimension.

Suppose we wish to load all values from 1 to 15 inclusive into TABLE giving the results shown in Fig. 7-7.

From this diagram we see that J refers to the rows and K to the columns. We wish to assign values 1-5 to row 1, values 6-10 to row 2, and 11-15 to row 3.

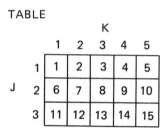

Fig. 7-7

Thus when J = 1, K must take on values 1-5. When J = 2, K repeats the values 1-5. Apparently a nested DØ will solve this problem. Since the assigned values are merely increments of 1, a simple counter N can be used to provide them.

```
N = 0
DØ J = 1 TØ 3;
DØ K = 1 TØ 5;
N = N+1;
TABLE(J,K) = N;
END;
END;
```

K, being the inner DØ, varies the fastest, thus all values are assigned to the first row before moving on to row 2 (i.e., J is then incremented).

To print the data from TABLE, a PUT statement within nested DØ loops could be used as follows:

```
DØ J = 1 TØ 3;
DØ K = 1 TØ 5;
PUT EDIT(TABLE(J,K))(SKIP,F(2));
END;
END;
```

This would print one element per line giving

1
2
3
4
5
6
7
8
9
10
11
12
13
14
15

Another method might be to print all elements on one line as follows:

```
DØ J = 1 TØ 3;
DØ K = 1 TØ 5;
PUT EDIT(TABLE(J,K))(F(3));
END;
END;
```

This gives as output

1 2 3 4 5 6 7 8 9 10 11 12 13 14 15

However, the output would be more attractive if it could be printed in a format similar to Fig. 7-7. This could be accomplished with the use of an indexed DØ statement.

Indexed Do

The indexed DØ functions like any other iterative DØ except that it is used as part of a GET or PUT data list.

```
PUT EDIT((SUMS(I) DØ I = 1 TØ 10),TØTAL)
    (10 F(4),F(6));
```

This statement causes 10 values of SUMS and the value of TØTAL to be printed on one output line.

Returning to the printing of TABLE we wish to print all values for each row on one line. Thus the statements

```
DØ J = 1 TØ 3;
PUT EDIT((TABLE(J,K) DØ K = 1 TØ 5))(SKIP,5 F(3));
END;
```

When J equals 1, K takes on values of 1 to 5 causing 5 elements from TABLE to print. When K reaches 5, J is increased by 1 and the process is continued. The output appears as follows:

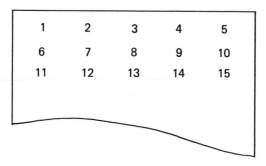

1	2	3	4	5
6	7	8	9	10
11	12	13	14	15

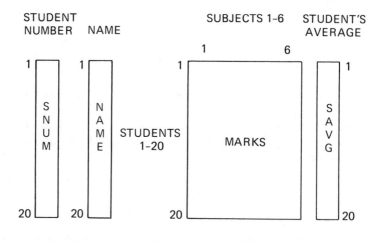

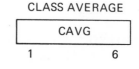

Fig. 7-8

Student and Class Averages

A program is required to compute each student's average for the subjects taken. The class average is also required for each subject. A pictorial representation of the arrays used might be as shown in Fig. 7–8.

Here four one-dimensional arrays and one two-dimensional array are used. SNUM stores the number of each student in a given class of 20 students. NAME stores the names of the students. MARKS contains the MARKS obtained by each of the students in each of the six subjects. SAVG will be used to compute each student's average and CAVG will be used to compute the class average for each subject. These arrays can be declared as follows:

```
DCL SNUM(20) FIXED(9), NAME(20) CHAR(15),
    MARKS(20,6) FIXED(2),
    SAVG(20) FIXED(4), CAVG(6) FIXED(4);
```

SAVG and CAVG are declared FIXED(4) since they will be used to develop a total prior to computing the average.

Assuming the class has exactly 20 students the data cards are read as follows:

```
DØ I = 1 TØ 20;
GET EDIT(SNUM(I),NAME(I),(MARKS(I,J)
        DØ J = 1 TØ 6))
        (SKIP,F(9),X(1),A(15),X(2),6F(2));
END;
```

The exterior DØ I = 1 TØ 20 controls the number of cards read. The indexed DØ J = 1 TØ 6 controls the reading of 6 MARKS per data card.

The next step in the program is to compute the average obtained by each student for the six subjects.

```
DØ I = 1 TØ 20;
SAVG(I) = 0;
DØ J = 1 TØ 6;
SAVG(I) = SAVG(I)+MARKS(I,J);
END;
SAVG(I) = SAVG(I)/6.0;
END;
```

The exterior DØ I = 1 TØ 20 sets position I of SAVG to 0. Then each mark is added into SAVG(I) for one student. When 6 MARKS have been accumulated, control passes out of the inner loop DØ J = 1 TØ 6. At this point the average is computed and stored in SAVG(I). This procedure is repeated 20 times, creating an average for each student.

The next routine computes the class average for each subject.

```
DØ I = 1 TØ 6;
CAVG(I) = 0;
DØ J = 1 TØ 20;
CAVG(I) = CAVG(I)+MARKS(J,I);
END;
CAVG(I) = CAVG(I)/20.0;
END;
```

This routine is almost identical to the student average computation except that it proceeds down each column first. When a complete subject has been processed, control passes to the next column of data and so on.

Figure 7-9 shows how these groups of statements look when combined into a composite program. Comments have been included to identify the purpose of each section of the program. To improve readability, statements within the nested DOs are indented. None of these things change the effectiveness of the program but rather make it easier to read and understand.

To complete this program, logic is needed to print the output. This is given as an assignment at the end of the chapter.

```
1  STUDENT:PROC OPTIONS(MAIN);
2  DCL SNUM(20) FIXED(9), NAME(20) CHAR(15),
       MARKS(20,6) FIXED(2),
       SAVG(20) FIXED(4), CAVG(6) FIXED(4);
   /* */
   /*** READ 20 MARKS CARDS INTO THE ARRAYS ***/
   /* */
3  DO I=1 TO 20;
4     GET EDIT (SNUM(I), NAME(I),(MARKS(I,J) DO J=1 TO 6))
             (SKIP,F(9),X(1),A(15),X(2),6 F(2));
5     END;
   /* */
   /***COMPUTE EACH STUDENT'S AVERAGE ***/
   /* */
6  DO I=1 TO 20;
7     SAVG(I)=0;
8     DO J=1 TO 6;
9        SAVG(I)=SAVG(I)+MARKS(I,J);
```

```
10        END;
11      SAVG(I)=SAVG(I)/6.0;
12      END;
      /* */
      /*** COMPUTE THE CLASS AVERAGE FOR EACH COURSE ***/
      /* */
13  DO I=1 TO 6;
14      CAVG(I)=0;
15      DO J=1 TO 20;
16          CAVG(I)=CAVG(I)+MARKS(J,I);
17      END;
18      CAVG(I)=CAVG(I)/20.0;
19      END;
20  END STUDENT;
```

Fig. 7-9

Three-Dimensional Arrays

The declare statement DCL PRØD(2,3,4) FIXED(2); reserves 24 storage positions, each capable of holding a two-digit number. Each element is accessible with the use of three subscripts. Figure 7-10 shows array PRØD.

PRØD

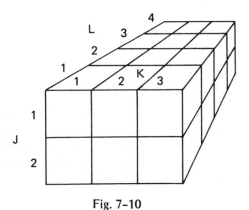

Fig. 7-10

In this diagram J,K,L represent the three dimensions. If we wished to assign to each element of the array the product of its subscripts, i.e., PRØD(1,1,1) receives 1(1x1x1), PRØD(1,1,2) receives 2(1x1x2), etc., nested DØ loops could be used as follows:

```
DØ J = 1 TØ 2;
DØ K = 1 TØ 3;
DØ L = 1 TØ 4;
PRØD(J,K,L) = J*K*L;
END;
END;
END;
```

These statements would assign the values 1 to 24 inclusive to each element of the array. Of course a counter such as was used for the two-dimensional program would produce similar results.

Sales by Month, Model and Region

To demonstrate the use of a three-dimensional array let's consider a computer manufacturer which sells ten different minicomputer models in three regions across the country. Data is provided for sales in each month in the following format:

1 - 2	Model
3 - 4	Month
5	Region
6 - 10	Sales(Dollars only)

There may be any number of cards for each model, month, and region. Furthermore, the cards are in no specific sequence. The objective of the program is to produce a report showing total dollar amounts in each month for every region and model. The sales for each month are to be on a separate page.

A solution to this problem is shown in Fig. 7-11 using a three-dimensional array to record the sales amounts. The first dimension represents the 10 models. The second represents the 12 months and the third dimension the 3 regions.

Statements 5 to 11 read the sales cards and add the sales amount to the appropriate element of the array. The model month and region from the card are used directly as subscripts when referencing the array,

```
1  COMP:PROC OPTIONS(MAIN);
2  DCL SALES(10,12,3)FIXED(6) INIT((360)0),
         (MODEL,MONTH) FIXED(2),
         REGION FIXED(1),
         AMOUNT FIXED(5),
```

```
     D CHAR(1) INIT(' ');
 3   DCL N FIXED(1) INIT(0);
 4   DCL TABLE(12) CHAR(9) INIT('JANUARY','FEBRUARY','MARCH',
                    'APRIL','MAY','JUNE','JULY',
                    'AUGUST','SEPTEMBER','OCTOBER',
                    'NOVEMBER', 'DECEMBER');
 5   ON ENDFILE(SYSIN) N=1;
 7   GET EDIT(MODEL,MONTH,REGION,AMOUNT)
               (2 F(2),F(1),F(5));
 8   DO WHILE(N=0);
 9        SALES(MODEL,MONTH,REGION)=SALES(MODEL,MONTH,RE-
          GION)+AMOUNT;
10      GET EDIT(MODEL,MONTH,REGION,AMOUNT)
               (COL(1),2 F(2),F(1),F(5));
11      END;
12   DO M=1 TO 12;
13      PUT EDIT(TABLE(M),'SALES') (PAGE,A(9),X(1),A);
14      PUT SKIP(2);
15      PUT EDIT('R E G I O N') (SKIP,COL(16),A)
               ('MODEL     1     2     3') (SKIP,A);
16      DO I=1 TO 10;
17        PUT EDIT(I) (SKIP,F(3));
18        PUT EDIT(D)(X(3),A(1));  /* DUMMY FIELD */
19        DO K=1 TO 3;
20           PUT EDIT(SALES(I,M,K)) (X(2),F(6));
21           END;
22        END;
23      END;
24   END COMP;
```

Fig. 7-11

Statements 12 to 23 print the contents of the array after all of the cards
have been recorded. The variable M is used to reference the 12 months of the
array Sales. It also serves a dual purpose by referencing the array TABLE which
contains the names of each of the 12 months. Depending on the value of M the
name of the month is directly selected from TABLE and used for each page
heading.

The variable I selects the model from the array as well as printing the
model number down the left side of the report. K is used for the region and controls the printing of each detail line of output.

The first page of output produced by this program is shown here. Examine it carefully and follow through the program to understand how the DO loops and subscripts are used to produce this report.

JANUARY SALES			
		R E G I O N	
MODEL	1	2	3
1	32000	30000	15000
2	20000	40000	0
3	0	0	0
4	0	0	50000
5	0	30000	60000
6	55000	4000	0
7	0	75500	0
8	15000	44560	12330
9	0	0	0
10	0	98000	0

Programming Problems

1. Read *n* values (maximum 100 values) into an array. Find and print the smallest and the largest number.

2. Read *n* values (max. 100). Sort them into ascending sequence without using another array. Print the sorted values.

3. Read and store a set of up to 50 table cards which contain product number and product name as follows:

    1- 3   Product Number
    4-15   Product Name

   Read data cards containing product number and associated data. Search for an equal product number in the table and print the name for that product. If no equal is found print the product number with 'NO EQUAL FOUND'.

4. A travel agency offers discounts on special travel packages. Each travel plan has a key number which is used to identify the destination and package discount. Special discounts are offered as follows:

Key	Destination	Discount
21	Miami	10%
27	Nassau	12%
39	Virgin Islands	10%

40	Hawaii	15%
45	Rio de Janeiro	20%
72	San Diego	12%

Each agency outlet supplies the following data.

1 -5	Customer Number
6 -20	Customer Name
21 -40	Customer Address
41 -46	Contract Price
47 -48	Package Key

Each record is to be read by the program and an array is searched for the Key. If an equal is not found, the contract price is printed in the report with an appropriate message. However, for keys found in the array, print the destination and the computed discount. Show all input data, the contract price, and the net price.

5. Complete the program in Fig. 7-9 by writing statements to print the output in a format similar to Fig. 7-8.

6. Grade cards are prepared by each college instructor in the following format:

1-9	Student Number
10-20	Student Name
21-25	Course Number
26-35	Course Name
36-38	Grade Received

Assuming that the cards are in sequence by course within student number, produce two types of reports. The first should have one page per student and show all courses taken by that student as well as the average of the grades. The second report, to be produced without resequencing or rereading the cards, should be a listing by course number showing the grades received in each course. For testing purposes use a small number of data cards.

7. A company has three warehouse locations. Goods are shipped from one of these warehouses to the customer. The warehouse chosen depends upon the shortest distance between that warehouse and the customer. This data is found in a mileage table with the following format:

DCL MILEAGE (3,20) FIXED (3);

The three-element dimension represents the warehouses and the second dimension the customer's city. Initialize this array to represent distances between cities in your geographical location.

Read the following data cards:

1-5	Customer No.
8-9	City Code
11-17	Cost of Goods (2 decimal)
18-21	Weight
22-35	Description

Find the closest warehouse to the customer. Based on the weight and distance compute the shipping charges. These are $0.15 per pound for each 50 miles of distance. There is a minimum charge of $1.00 for shipping. Produce an appropriate report.

8. Produce a calendar for the current year. Use one two-dimensional array and print one month per page.

9. Produce a calendar using a three-dimensional array. Print the entire year on one page.

10. Given data cards containing product number, supplier and unit cost find and print the supplier with the lowest cost for each product. There are *n* products with no more than five suppliers per product.

1-3	Product Number
4-6	Supplier
7-11	Unit Cost

11. The users of the sales program in Fig. 7-11 have found that the model, month, and region in the data cards have not always been valid. Specifically they are sometimes outside of the range of values allowed. Modify the program to edit these fields and reject cards containing errors. Produce an error report showing the card in error and a message identifying the type of error(s).

In addition to this, several other reports are required.

a. A list of sales by model showing region and month sales within each model.

b. A summary report listing total sales by month.

c. A summary report listing total sales by region within model. There should be no individual monthly values shown.

12. An electronics firm has 9 salesmen. During the month each earned a basic

salary plus a commission as shown on the data cards. Each salesman also recorded the number of calls made during that month.

1–3	Salesman Number
4–7	Basic Salary (Dollars only)
8–11	Commission (Dollars only)
12–14	Calls made

Compute the average number of calls made and the average gross salary. Print each saleman's data and show the difference between his calls and the average number of calls. Also show the difference between the gross salary for each salesman and the average gross salary. These differences could be positive or negative values.

13. A company employs less than 200 employees in the data processing division. The ages of these employees are recorded on data cards. Produce a report showing the average age, the median and the mode. *Note:* The median is the number found at the midpoint when the numbers are sequenced. The median of 21,23,23,25,28,29,30 is 25. The mode is the number which occurs most frequently. In this case 23 is the mode.

14. An insurance company provides an annuity for life on a life insurance policy. Payments are based on the following table, based on a $1,000 face value policy.

LIFE INCOME

Age when Annuity Begins		Life	10 Years	20 Years
Male	Female	Annuity	Certain	Certain
40	45	3.95	3.80	3.73
45	50	4.20	4.02	3.98
50	55	4.63	4.51	4.40
55	60	5.27	5.12	4.85
60	65	5.90	5.65	5.15
65	70	6.95	6.38	5.85

A policy holder may choose an annuity to extend for life (until the death of the policy holder), for 10 years guaranteed (even if he dies, payments continue), or 20 years guaranteed.

For instance, if Mr. Gerry Johnson is age 55, and decides to accept a life annuity on a $10,000 policy, he will receive 10 times 5.27 or $52.70 per month for life.

Read a number of cards in the following format and determine payments to be made to each policy holder. Print the policy number, name, face value, payment category (Life, 10 years, or 20 years), and monthly payments.

1-5	Policy Number	
6	Payment Category	1. Life Annuity
		2. 10 Years
		3. 20 Years
7-13	Face Value (Dollars Only)	
14	Sex - M- Male	
	F- Female	
15-29	Name of Policy Holder	
30-31	Age	

8

Internal and External Procedures

Good program organization is a vital part of each programmer's task. It not only makes for a neater looking program but facilitates debugging of the program as well as making program revisions after implementation much easier.

The use of procedures, in addition to the main procedure, usually assists in organizing a program in a beneficial manner. Procedures increase programming efficiency by permitting commonly used routines to be written once and then executed whenever they are required.

Internal Procedure

The general format for internal procedure is shown in Fig. 8-1.

```
A:PRØCEDURE ØPTIONS(MAIN);

B:PRØCEDURE(parameter 1, parameter 2, etc);

END B;
END A;
```

Fig. 8-1

In Fig. 8-1, B is an internal procedure contained within main procedure A. The beginning of B is determined by the presence of the PRØCEDURE statement. The end of the procedure is identified by the END statement. The label B referenced in the end is optional. Notice that procedure B is completely contained within procedure A. This is essential, and there can be no overlapping. The *parameter* list is optional and may be omitted if desired. Procedure B may contain any valid PL/I statements such as have been covered in previous chapters.

Invocation Using a Call

An internal procedure is activated by the execution of a CALL statement. Refer to Fig. 8-2 for the general format.

---

label:CALL *Procedure Name* (*argument 1,*
                              argument 2, etc);

Fig. 8-2

label	Follows the rules for statement labels. May be referenced by any program control statement. The *label* is optional.
CALL	Keyword specifying that a PRØCEDURE is to be activated.
Procedure Name	The name of the procedure which is being activated by this CALL.
(*argument 1, argument 2, etc.*)	A list of arguments. These are variable names representing data which may be used in the called procedure. Arguments are optional. When used argument 1 corresponds to parameter 1, argument 2 to parameter 2, and so on, in the procedure called.

The CALL statement causes control to be passed from the CALL itself (the *point of invocation*) to the procedure named. This change in program control is similar to the execution of a GØ TØ statement. The essential difference is that when the procedure is completed, control will automatically return to the statement following the *point of invocation*.

Termination

An internal procedure is terminated when the END statement is encountered during program execution. Control is passed back to the statement following the CALL statement which *invoked* the procedure.

Return Statement

The RETURN statement permits the termination of a procedure at points other than the end of the procedure. Figure 8-3 shows the general format. The label is optional.

label:RETURN;

Fig. 8-3

Figure 8-4 shows how an internal procedure may be invoked from various places from within the main procedure. When B is called from statement 08, control is transferred to statement 24. If X was greater than Y, then statements 28 to 33 are executed. Since a RETURN is encountered before the END of the DØ group control passes from statement 33 to the statement following the CALL (09).

```
01      A:PRØC ØPTIONS(MAIN);
            .
            .
            .
08      CALL B;
09          .
            .
            .
17      CALL B;
18          .
            .
23          .
24      B:PRØC;
            .
            .
            .
28      IF  X>Y THEN DØ;
            .
            .
            .
33      RETURN;
34      END;
35      IF  X = Y THEN DØ;
            .
            .
```

```
42     │   RETURN;
43     │   END;
       │     .
       │     .
       │     .
51     │   END B;
52     │   END A;
```

Fig. 8–4

If X equals Y then ultimately control leaves B from statement 42. If X was less than Y control would return from statement 51. Thus statements 33, 42, and 51 all have the same effect of returning control back to the statement following the point of invocation.

If B had been invoked from statement 17, all returns would be to statement 18 upon termination of procedure B.

External Procedure

External procedures are similar to internal procedures in use and organization. The primary difference is that they are physically external to the main procedure. They are invoked in the same manner as internal procedures and are terminated in the same way. External procedures may also contain internal procedures. The general format of an external procedure is shown in Fig. 8–5.

```
A:PRØC ØPTIONS(MAIN);
  .
  .
  .
END A;
B:PRØC;
  .
  .
  .
END B;
```

Fig. 8–5

Nesting

Figure 8–6 shows a main procedure with a number of internal procedures. When a procedure contains another procedure within it, it is called nesting. Since

Procedure A contains B, procedure B is nested within A. A is considered to be at level 1 whereas B is at level 2 of nesting. C is also contained in A and is also at level 2. D is contained within C and is therefore at level 3 of nesting. The number of levels permitted depends upon the compiler used. The number of internal procedures permitted is also restricted by the compiler. This limit is, however, beyond normal programming requirements and does not generally impose any restrictions upon the programmer.

In Fig. 8-6, A or B may invoke procedure C. C may invoke B provided B is not presently active. C may call D but A and B may not. A, B, and C could invoke an external procedure if one were present. Any internal procedures contained within an external procedure may only be invoked from within the external procedure following the above rules.

```
A:PRØC ØPTIONS(MAIN);
  .
  .
  .
  B:PRØC;
    .
    .
    .
  END B;
  C:PRØC;
    .
    .
    .
    D:PRØC;
      .
      .
      .
    END D;
  END C;
END A;
```

Fig. 8-6

Entry

Previously, all procedures were activated by calling the procedure name which transferred control to the beginning of that procedure. With entry points it is possible to begin execution at different points within the procedure. Figure 8-7 shows an internal procedure X1 containing entry points X2 and X3. Procedure X1 may be activated by issuing a CALL for X1 or X2 or X3. Depending upon the label used, control is passed on to the appropriate point in the internal procedure. When a RETURN or END is encountered control passes back to the point of invocation.

```
A:PRØC ØPTIONS(MAIN);

CALL X1;

CALL X2;

CALL X3;

X1:PRØC;

X2:ENTRY;

X3:ENTRY;

END X1;
END A;
```

Fig. 8–7

When the internal procedure is executing and the ENTRY statement is encountered, it is ignored. Thus it is useful only as an alternate entry point to the procedure.

Some useful applications for internal procedures are:

1. Reading files and checking sequence

2. Heading routines

3. Total routines

4. Error routines

5. Editing functions

6. General calculations commonly used throughout the main program.

Invoice Report

Figure 8–8 shows a program using internal procedures to produce an Invoice Report. This is a listing showing all purchases by customer with a total for each customer. Input data is in the following format:

1-6	Customer Number
7-12	Part Number
13-17	Unit Cost
18-22	Quantity

Main Program Logic

1. On endfile print customer total (CTOT)
        print overall total

2. Print headings(HEAD)

3. Read card(READC)

4. Process until end of file

    4.1 If same customer number then
            calculate total cost
            print detail line
            add 1 to line count

        4.1.1 If line count exceeds 25 then print heading(HEAD)

        4.1.2 Add total cost to customer total

        4.1.3 Read card(READC)

    4.2 If change of customer number then
            print customer total(CTOT)
            store customer number

Procedures

1. READC

    1.1 Read card

    1.2 If customer number less than previous then print 'seq error'
                                            stop

2. HEAD

    2.1 Print heading lines 1 and 2

    2.2 Skip a line

    2.3 Set line count to zero

3. CTOT

    3.1 Print customer total line

3.2 Add customer total to overall total

3.3 Set customer total to zero

3.4 Skip 3 lines

    The program utilizes three internal procedures. READC is used to read the data cards and check the customer number sequence. If a sequence error occurs, a message is printed and the program is terminated in this procedure.

    HEAD prints the headings at the top of the report. Also if a page exceeds 25 lines of data, HEAD is invoked and a new page is begun with a heading.

    CTOT is used to print the Customer Total. It also adds the total to OTOTAL. This represents the overall total to be printed at the end of the report. CTOT is called whenever the customer number changes as well as at end of file. This last call is necessary to get a total for the final customer on the report.

```
1  INVOICE:PROC OPTIONS(MAIN);
2  DCL  (CNO,PART) FIXED(6),
          UNIT FIXED(5,2),
          QTY FIXED(5),
          PCNO FIXED(6) INIT(0),
          TOTAL FIXED(7,2) INIT(0),
          CTOTAL FIXED(8,2) INIT(0),
          OTOTAL FIXED(9,2) INIT(0);
3  DCL  LINE FIXED(2) INIT(0),
          N     FIXED(1) INIT(0);
   /* */
   /* MAINLINE LOGIC */
   /* */
4  ON ENDFILE(SYSIN) BEGIN;
6     CALL CTOT;
7     PUT EDIT('OVERALL  TOTAL',OTOTAL)(SKIP(3),X(29),
       A,F(10,2));
8     PUT PAGE;
9     STOP;
10    END;
11 CALL HEAD;
12 CALL READC;
13 PCNO=CNO;
14 DO WHILE(N=0);
15    IF CNO=PCNO THEN DO;
17       TOTAL=UNIT*QTY;
```

```
18    PUT EDIT(CNO,PART,UNIT,QTY,TOTAL)
              (SKIP,X(1),F(6),X(5),F(6),X(6),F(6,2),X(5),
              F(5),X(5)
              ,F(8,2));
19    LINE=LINE+1;
20    IF LINE>=25 THEN CALL HEAD;
22    CTOTAL=CTOTAL+TOTAL;
23    CALL READC;
24    END;
25  IF CNO>PCNO THEN DO;
27    CALL CTOT;
28    PCNO=CNO;
29    END;
30  END;
31  READC:PROC;
32  GET EDIT(CNO,PART,UNIT,QTY)
              (COL(1),F(6),F(6),F(5,2),F(5));
33  IF CNO<PCNO THEN DO;
35    PUT EDIT ('SEQUENCE ERROR IN ',CNO) (SKIP,A,
      F(6));
36    STOP; /* TERMINATE RUN */
37    END;
38  END;

39  HEAD:PROC;
40  PUT EDIT('INVOICE REPORT')(PAGE,X(20),A);
41  PUT EDIT('CUSTOMER  PART NUMBER  UNIT COST
    QUANTITY  TOTAL COST')
              (SKIP(2),A);
42  PUT SKIP;
43  LINE=0;
44  END;

45  CTOT:PROC;
46  PUT EDIT('CUSTOMER TOTAL',CTOTAL) (SKIP(2),X(29),
    A,F(10,2));
47  OTOTAL=OTOTAL+CTOTAL;
48  CTOTAL=0;
49  PUT SKIP(3);
50  END;

51  END INVOICE;
```

Fig. 8–8

The program was run using the following data as input:

```
230122 1234560100000005
2301222334500040000100
2455001234560100000015
2455002223000007504500
2455005555550250000010
```

The output produced is shown below. Since there were only a few input cards, the output did not exceed 25 lines. Thus HEAD was only invoked once for the first page.

INVOICE REPORT				
CUSTOMER	PART NUMBER	UNIT COST	QUANTITY	TOTAL COST
230122	123456	10.00	5	50.00
230122	233450	4.00	100	400.00
			CUSTOMER TOTAL	450.00
245500	123456	10.00	15	150.00
245500	222300	0.75	4500	3375.00
245500	555555	25.00	10	250.00
			CUSTOMER TOTAL	3775.00
			OVERALL TOTAL	4225.00

Internal Attribute

Variables may be declared within internal procedures using the methods described in Chapter 3. Where these variables may be referenced depends upon whether they include the INTERNAL or EXTERNAL attribute.

When INTERNAL is used, the variable will be known only within the procedure in which it is declared. Figure 8-9 shows how these attributes are used in a PL/I program.

```
A:PRØC ØPTIONS(MAIN);

    DCL VALUE FIXED(7,2),N CHAR(10),
        AMT FIXED(5) EXTERNAL,

    CALL B;
```

```
    CALL C;

B:PRØC;

    DCL SUM BINARY FIXED(6) INTERNAL,
        N BIT(5) INTERNAL,
        TØT FIXED(6,3) EXTERNAL;

    END B;

END A;

    C:PRØC;

    DCL AMT FIXED(5)EXTERNAL,
        TØT FIXED(6,3)EXTERNAL,
        N FIXED(1) INTERNAL;
    END C;
```

Fig. 8-9

In procedure B, SUM and N are declared as INTERNAL and may therefore be processed only within B. Procedure A contains a variable N. However, it will not be considered the same variable N as in B since the second declare of N defines it as internal to B. Thus the use of N will reference different storage locations depending upon its use in A or B. N has also been declared as INTERNAL in C. This refers to a third storage location which will only be accessible by the use of variable N in C.

VALUE is declared in A and since A contains B and VALUE is not a declare within B, this variable may be referenced within either procedure A or B. Thus the use of VALUE will always refer to the same variable.

External Attribute

When a variable is to be available in more than one external procedure (including MAIN), the EXTERNAL attribute is used to make this variable accessible. A variable with the EXTERNAL attribute is known in all procedures where it is declared as external. In the D-level compiler external names are limited to six characters in length. Files are external by default but must be declared in each external procedure in which they are used.

Figure 8-9 shows an example of the use of the EXTERNAL attribute. AMT is declared as external in A and in C. Reference to AMT in either procedure accesses the same variable.

TØT is declared as external in B and C. It will be available in either of these procedures during program execution time.

Storage Class

Static and Automatic Attributes

In addition to the INTERNAL attribute for variable declares, the STATIC and AUTOMATIC attributes may be used. All EXTERNAL variables are assumed to be STATIC so it makes little sense to include this attribute with EXTERNAL.

When dealing with internally declared variables we know that the variable is available only within the procedure in which it is declared. When the procedure is terminated, what happens to the contents of the variable depends upon the storage class chosen.

STATIC causes the contents of the variable to remain static or unchanged when the containing procedure is terminated. Upon returning to the procedure at a later time during program execution, we can expect to find the same value in the variable that had originally been placed there.

AUTØMATIC, on the other hand, releases the storage used by the variable when the procedure is terminated. This storage may now be used in other procedures for other AUTØMATIC variables. Thus when control returns to procedure, the contents of AUTØMATIC variables will be unpredictable.

AUTØMATIC is particularly useful for temporary storage requirements within a procedure. For instance, an array may be used to develop certain values. Once the results are available the array is no longer required outside of the procedure. Thus AUTØMATIC releases the storage for other use. In other cases the results of the computation may be needed again upon return to the procedure and may therefore be declared as STATIC.

Validity Checking

The programs used in this text have always assumed that correct data has been supplied. However, this is not always the case. There can be many reasons for invalid data such as keypunch errors, correct data but in the wrong field, a misunderstanding about what kind of data is required, and so on. By anticipating the kinds of errors which might occur, we can develop program logic to detect these errors.

Numeric Errors

One of the most common types of errors occurs when a numeric field does not contain all numeric digits. For instance 2309 is punched as 23O9 in the data card. An efficient method to detect this in PL/1 is to examine each character of the field to determine if it is a numeric digit. This can be done using the SUBSTR built-in function to examine each byte of the field separately. Since nonnumeric characters such as letters and special characters are less than numbers it is sufficient to compare each character to zero. Anything less than zero is invalid.

Using this concept we will now write an internal procedure in Fig. 8-10 to check any field supplied to it for numeric. This is the first parameter FIELD. The second parameter gives the length of the field to be tested and is called LENGTH. The third parameter TYPE provides an alphabetic description of the field (such as 'PART NO.') to be used in an error message. The procedure is initiated by a call such as CALL NUM(ACCOUNT,5, 'ACCOUNT NO.');

```
01  NUM:PROC(FIELD,LENGTH,TYPE);
02  DCL  FIELD CHAR(5),
           LENGTH FIXED(1),
           TYPE CHAR(12) ;
03  DO I=1 TO  LENGTH;
04      IF  SUBSTR(FIELD,I,1) < '0' THEN DO;
05          PUT EDIT('NON NUMERIC CHAR(S)  IN ',TYPE)
                    (COL(40),A,A(12));
06          PUT SKIP;
07          I=LENGTH; /* FORCED END OF LOOP */
08          END;
09      END;
10  END NUM;
```

Fig. 8-10

The DO loop varies I from 1 to the last character in the field provided by LENGTH. If the field is 3 bytes long then LENGTH contains 3 and only three characters will be tested for numeric.

Within the DO, an IF statement uses the SUBSTR function to compare each character to 0. Characters which are greater than or equal to zero are numeric and the DO simply continues to the next character. A less than condition causes the error message to be printed including TYPE which contains the name of the field in error. The loop is then terminated.

Figure 8-11 shows an edit program which uses the procedure NUM to edit a card containing five numeric fields. The essential mainline of the program consists of statements 7 to 15. In this section, each card is processed by calling NUM for each field in the card. In each case the field, its length, and its description is supplied to NUM and editing occurs. If an error is found in one field a message is printed and control is passed to the next call. Thus all fields are edited regardless of the number of errors.

Another important consideration is that each field is declared as character. If they had been fixed, a conversion error would have occurred in the GET and the program terminated.

```
01  EDIT:PROC OPTIONS(MAIN);
02  DCL  (PART,ORDER,EMPLOYEE) CHAR(5),
          QTY CHAR(4),
          HOURS CHAR(3),
          N FIXED(1) INIT(1);

03  ON ENDFILE(SYSIN)STOP;
05  CALL HEAD;
06  CALL READC;

07  DO WHILE(N=1);
08      PUT EDIT(PART,ORDER,QTY,HOURS,EMPLOYEE)
                (SKIP(2),A(5),X(3),A(5),X(3),A(4),X(3),A(3),
                X(4),A(5));
09      CALL NUM(PART,5,'PART NO.');
10      CALL NUM(ORDER,5,'ORDER NO.');
11      CALL NUM(QTY,4,'QUANTITY');
12      CALL NUM(HOURS,3,'HOURS');
13      CALL NUM(EMPLOYEE,5,'EMPLOYEE NO.');
14      CALL READC;
15      END;

16      HEAD:PROC;
17          PUT EDIT('JOB REPORTING CARDS EDIT')
                    (PAGE,X(11),A);
18          PUT EDIT (' PART  ORDER  QTY  HOURS  EMPLOYEE',
                      'ERROR') (SKIP(2),A,COL(47),A);
19          END;

20      READC:PROC;
21          GET  EDIT(PART,ORDER,QTY,HOURS,EMPLOYEE)
                     (COL(1),2 A(5),A(4),A(3),A(5));
22          END;
23      NUM:PROC(FIELD,LENGTH,TYPE);
24      DCL  FIELD CHAR(5) ,
             LENGTH FIXED(1),
             TYPE CHAR(12);
25      DO I=1 TO LENGTH;
26          IF  SUBSTR(FIELD,I,1) < '0' THEN DO;
```

```
28              PUT EDIT('NON NUMERIC CHAR(S)  IN ',TYPE)
                    (COL(40),A,A(12));
29              PUT SKIP;
30              I=LENGTH;  /* FORCED END OF LOOP */
31          END;
32        END;
33      END NUM;

34    END EDIT;
```

JOB REPORTING CARDS EDIT					
PART	ORDER	QTY	HOURS	EMPLOYEE	ERROR
12345	23A44	0004	100	45678	NON NUMERIC CHAR(S) IN ORDER NO.
23345	26000	0250	025	34511	
A2300	67&'8	45	3.5	88S99	NON NUMERIC CHAR(S) IN PART NO.
					NON NUMERIC CHAR(S) IN ORDER NO.
					NON NUMERIC CHAR(S) IN QUANTITY
					NON NUMERIC CHAR(S) IN HOURS
					NON NUMERIC CHAR(S) IN EMPLOYEE NO.
35500	60000	0500	030	05675	
35670	23#33	0067	055	#4550	NON NUMERIC CHAR(S) IN ORDER NO.
					NON NUMERIC CHAR(S) IN EMPLOYEE NO.

Fig. 8-11

Several interesting questions arise from this problem.

1. What needs to be changed to allow for numeric fields of up to 10 digits?

2. How could hours be used in an arithmetic calculation after it was determined to be numeric?

3. How could an array be used profitably for the field names?

4. For field lengths?

5. If there were numerous fields, say 15, would 15 calls be necessary? Could an array be used to reduce this to one call?

These problems will be dealt with in the programming exercises at the end of the chapter.

Alphabetic Errors

This is an error similar in type to a numeric error except that alphabetic characters are required. A procedure similar to NUM could be used and each character would be tested for alphabetic. Since special characters are less than A and numeric digits are greater than Z a test for characters between A and Z inclusive would solve the problem.

Range

This test is used when a specific field must consist of values between certain limits. A code may be any of the values 10 to 15. You might first test code for numeric and then check for the range 10 to 15. Values below or above these would be invalid.

Names could also be batched by their first letter, so that a given group of data may contain the range of names from A to I. All names beginning with these letters are correct, all others are in the wrong batch. An alphabetic test of the field could be done followed by a test of the first letter of the name.

Missing Data

Generally this is caught by one of the other tests. It usually is simply a blank field.

Combination of Fields

This test involves examining two or more fields for validity. For instance in a date field you might test month for the range 1 to 12. After determining the valid month, this can in turn be used to determine the correct range for day. January (month 1) can only have days 1 to 31, February has 28 (except on leap year), and so on.

Not every program will require all of the checks listed here but it is never wise to assume data will be correct. Most tests are fairly simple and will certainly pay off in detecting errors which might otherwise terminate the program.

Programming Problems

1. Read data cards in the following format:

1-2	Region Number
3-10	Vendor Number
11-17	Item Number
18-30	Description
31-37	Unit Cost (2 decimal)
38-44	Quantity

Produce a Vendor Purchase Report in the format shown. Sequence check cards on Item Number within Vendor Number within Region Number (*Hint:*

use concatenation). There may be any number of cards per vendor, thus page overflow for headings is required. Page numbers begin at 1 for each region.

   At the end of each vendor, print a total for all purchases from that vendor. A separate page is required at the end showing a total of each region and an overall total. There are a maximum of 10 regions.

```
┌─────────────────────────────────────────────────────────────────────┐
│                    VENDOR PURCHASE REPORT                             │
│                                                                       │
│                                                  PAGE 1               │
│           REGION 01                   VENDOR NUMBER 43012155          │
│    ITEM                         UNIT                      TOTAL        │
│    NUMBER        DESCRIPTION    COST    QUANTITY          COST         │
│    0367815       CLAMP          1.50     100             150.00        │
│    0428110       BRACKET        2.25      10              22.50        │
│    0739337       FRAME         75.10      20            1502.00        │
│                                                                       │
│                                 VENDOR TOTAL            1674.50        │
│                                                                       │
└──────────────                                       ──────────────────┘
```

2. A local major department store has a credit policy whereby your monthly payment decreases as the amount still due on your account decreases. The rate of interest on your account is calculated at 1½ percent per month on the highest unpaid balance within that month. Monthly payments are determined as follows:

PAYMENT SCALE	AMOUNT	MONTHLY PAYMENT
	100.00	5.00
	150.00	6.50
	200.00	7.50
	250.00	9.00
	300.00	11.00
	350.00	12.50
	400.00	14.50

Possible data might be as follows:

Current unpaid balance – $344.42

Purchases – Month 2   – $ 43.98
Month 3   – $ 10.00
Month 12 – $ 5.10
Month 17 – $ 40.68

As a consumer I wish to know the following information:

a. If my purchases are as shown, and I adhere strictly to the Payment Scale table, how many months would it take for me to close my account, what would my overall interest rate be, and what would be my final payment to close this account?

b. If I chose to ignore the declining monthly payment, and paid monthly at the maximum payment required at the maximum value of my unpaid balance, how many months would it take for me to close my account, what would my overall interest rate be, and what would be my final payment to close this account?

Write a PL/1 program to supply the above answers, allowing for:

1. Variable initial unpaid balance.

2. A maximum of 10 purchases to be considered over the span of the account.

3. Unpaid balances in excess of $400.00 are paid at the rate of $14.50.

Design your own input card format and output report format.

3. Canadian Income Tax Return Calculation
A program is to be written to calculate Federal and Provincial Income Tax based on a simplified version of the T1 Short Tax Return. The input data, one card per taxpayer, is in the following format:

A	1- 9	Social Insurance Number
B	10-16	Total Earnings
C	17-21	Canada Pension Contribution
D	22-26	Registered Pension
E	27-33	Income Tax Deducted
F	34-39	Other Deductions
G	40-46	Personal Deductions
H	47-52	Medical or Charitable
I	53-58	Date

(Fields B-H are all 2 decimal.)

a. Determine Taxable Income.

Taxable Income = B - (C+D+F+G+H)

Note 1: C must be adjusted to compensate for Canada Pension Overpayment. This is determined by calculating 1.8% of TOTAL Earnings. If contributions exceed this amount refund the difference. The maximum allowable contribution is $84.60.

b. Detailed Tax Calculation.

    1. Basic Tax is determined by the following table.

$ 1,000 or less	11%		
1,000	$ 110 + 14% on next	$ 1,000	
2,000	250 + 17%	″	1,000
3,000	420 + 19%	″	1,000
4,000	610 + 22%	″	2,000
6,000	1,050 + 26%	″	2,000
8,000	1,570 + 30%	″	2,000
10,000	2,170 + 35%	″	2,000
12,000	2,870 + 40%	″	3,000
15,000	4,070 + 45%	″	10,000

    2. Federal Abatements
       Provincial Abatement: 28% of Basic Tax
       Tax Reduction: 20% of Basic Tax
                      (maximum of $20.00)

    3. Surtax: 3% of (Basic Tax – $200.00)

    4. Old Age Security: 6% of Taxable Income (maximum of $360.00)

    5. Provincial Income Tax: 28% of Basic Tax

Note 2: Federal Tax is Basic Tax – Abatements + Surtax + Security. Total Tax is Federal Tax + Provincial Tax.

c. Produce the following report showing the results of the calculations and whether additional tax is payable or whether a refund may be claimed. The last line of output would indicate either AMOUNT OWING, as in the example, or TAX PAYABLE.

INCOME TAX RETURN

SOCIAL INSURANCE NUMBER 570 121 300

TOTAL EARNINGS   25000.00

DEDUCTIONS

CANADA PENSION	100.00	
OVERPAYMENT	15.40	84.60
REGISTERED PENSION		300.00
OTHER DEDUCTIONS		50.00
PERSONAL EXEMPTIONS		1000.00
MEDICAL OR CHARITABLE		0.00

TOTAL DEDUCTIONS   1434.60

TAXABLE INCOME   23565.40

TAX CALCULATION

         ON FIRST   15000.00 TAX IS   4070.00
         ON REM'G   8565.40 TAX IS   3854.43
                         BASIC TAX IS   7924.43

PROVINCIAL ABATEMENT   2218.84
TAX REDUCTION   20.00
SURTAX   231.73
OLD AGE SECURITY   360.00

FEDERAL TAX PAYABLE   6277.32

PROVINCIAL TAX PAYABLE   2218.84

TOTAL TAX PAYABLE   8496.16

TOTAL TAX DEDUCTED   3000.00

OVERPAYMENT   15.40   8480.76

         AMOUNT OWING   5480.76

4. Write a program to edit the Income Tax cards from the previous problem
   for possible errors. The program is to produce an error report listing only
   the cards in error. Each card is to appear only once with a list of error
   messages pertaining to it. All errors in a card must be found. Don't stop at
   the first one. The following errors are to be detected:
   a. Every field must be numeric. Check each field separately and use a
      unique error message for each one.
   b. Total Earnings must not exceed $25000.00.
   c. No negative values are permitted.
   d. The total of the deductions should not exceed the Total Earnings.
   e. Data is in the form MMDDYY. Month must be in the range 01 to 12.
      Day must correspond to the limits for the indicated month. Year will
      be the current tax year.

   Use arrays to store the error messages, field locations and field lengths. This
   can be used for most of the editing. However, a slight deviation from this
   may be necessary when testing the range of values.

5. A large wholesale outlet is planning to change the unit of measure presently used on many of its items to a new unit of measure. Unit of measure is identified by code as follows:

01	Units	06	CWT
02	Dozens	07	Tons
03	Gross	08	Inches
04	Ounces	09	Feet
05	Pounds	10	Yards

Write a program to convert each data record from the existing U/M to the new U/M. Produce a report identifying existing quantities and unit cost and a new quantity and unit cost under the new U/M. Edit the data for possible invalid change. For example a change from U/M 01-03 to 08-10 or 01-03 to 04-07.

1-7	Part Number
8-9	Present Unit of Measure
10-11	Convert to U/M
12-18	Quantity
19-26	Unit Cost (3 decimal)
27-40	Description

9

Record Input/Output

This chapter on the use of record files and the following chapter on indexed sequential will be of primary interest to users of the D and F compilers and the PL/I Optimizer. As of the writing of this text, PL/C has not made provision for these areas of the PL/I language.

In Chapter 5 the processing of data using files external to the program was discussed. This stream approach to file processing presents several limitations to the PL/I programmer. One of these restrictions is that blocked records on files such as disk or tape cannot be used. The nature of these devices is that they seldom operate efficiently unless several logical records are blocked into one physical record.

A second disadvantage of stream relates to the conversions required of each data item when it is read from the hardware device and placed in the declared variable. These conversions require a certain amount of processing time and thus reduce the operating efficiency of the PL/I program. The ease with which stream may be used sometimes outweighs these disadvantages. However, in most business applications, it is preferable to use the RECØRD concept for processing files because of increased operating efficiency and effective storage utilization.

Structures

When using record oriented processing the program no longer reads individual data items as it did for stream. As the term record implies, the program accesses

159

a logical record in its entirety. Since a complete record is accessed, no conversion of individual data items is performed. This means that the programmer must ensure that the declare written corresponds directly to the way data is stored in the device.

Since a complete record is read, the declared variables must be grouped together. This grouping is called a structure. All records from a given file will be read into the structure as they are required. The structure is capable of holding one logical record at a time.

Figure 9-1 shows a schematic representation of a data card in the following format:

1-20	Surname
21-23	Initials
24-45	Street
46-60	City
61-70	Province
71-76	Date
77-80	Unused

1	CARD							
2	NAME		ADDRESS			DATE		UNUSED
3	SURNAME	INITIALS	STREET	CITY	PROV	MONTH	DAY	YEAR

Fig. 9-1

We see that the card in its entirety is represented by level number 1 which then includes all subsequent data elements. Level number 2 shows a more detailed breakdown of the card, giving name, address, etc. Level number 3 breaks down level 2 items into even more detail. Thus name is divided into surname and initials. Notice that the unused field is not broken down into a third level. It is already described in full detail at level 2.

This breakdown could proceed to a fourth or greater levels if the nature of the data made this necessary. Of course data may be fully defined at level 2 and need not proceed to a further level.

What has been shown in Fig. 9-1 is a structure of the data record. CARD is called a *major structure* since it contains all the items of the record within it. NAME, ADDRESS and DATE are *minor structures* since they are broken down to further level of definition. SURNAME, INITIALS, STREET, CITY, PRØV,

MØNTH, DAY, YEAR, and UNUSED are all *elementary names* since they have no further breakdown. Notice that the level number has nothing to do with the minor structure or elementary name. Rather, it relates to the way the field is defined.

In PL/I this structure would be declared as shown in Fig. 9-2. Notice that only elementary names receive the defining attributes for the fields. The major and minor structures are used to position them within the record. Each elementary name appears under the structure it is contained in. MONTH, DAY, and YEAR are grouped in brackets since their level number and attributes are the same. DATE could have been declared as:

```
2 DATE,
   3 MØNTH      CHAR(2),
   3 DAY        CHAR(2),
   3 YEAR       CHAR(2),
```

however the former approach is easier for the programmer.

```
DCL   1    CARD,
           2  NAME,
              3  SURNAME  CHAR(20),
              3  INITIALS  CHAR(3),
           2  ADDRESS,
              3  STREET   CHAR(22),
              3  CITY     CHAR(15),
              3  PRØV     CHAR(10),
           2  DATE,
              3  (MØNTH,DAY,YEAR)    CHAR(2),
           2  UNUSED    CHAR(4);
```

Fig. 9-2

The indenting of different level numbers in the structure is for the convenience of the programmer. It is not a requirement of the language.

As stated previously, records are read into structures without any data conversion taking place. In the case of the structure in Fig. 9-2, this would not present any particular difficulties since the attribute CHAR reflects a zoned decimal field. However, if we were to read numeric information from this card, a zoned decimal field would be read from the card but the FIXED attribute would expect to read packed decimal information. Since there is a discrepancy between the card input which is zoned decimal and the attribute in the structure which would be FIXED, a data conversion would not occur. Therefore, we need an attribute which can read numeric information as zoned decimal. First let us look at a brief description of zoned and packed decimals.

Zoned and Packed Decimal

The terms *zoned* and *packed* refer to the way data is stored in main storage in the System/370. Zoned refers to character information but it is quite commonly used to record numeric information as well. Packed decimal is related only to the storing of numeric information which ultimately will be used for some type of calculation.

Figure 9-3 shows the general format used internally for a zoned decimal field. This diagram shows a series of four bytes stored internally in System/370. A byte is the term used to represent a storage location. Each byte is divided into two basic sections, a zone portion and a decimal portion. The former section contains a zone which defines whether the information stored is alphabetic, special character, or numeric. The decimal portion indicates the numeric value of the field.

Fig. 9-3   *Zoned Decimal*

Figure 9-4 shows a packed decimal field. If the data from Fig. 9-3 were stored in packed format, assuming the data were numeric, the right-most byte would be stored in the right-most byte of the packed decimal field. The digit from the zoned field would be stored in the left portion of this byte. The zone would be converted to a sign and stored in the units position. Each subsequent digit from the zoned decimal field would then be stored in related halves of the packed field.

Fig. 9-4   *Packed Decimal*

Note that 4 bytes of zoned data can be stored in 3 bytes of packed digits. In fact, 5 bytes may be stored in 3.

The PL/I attribute FIXED DECIMAL relates to packed decimal fields and any reference to a fixed decimal field in PL/I refers internally to a packed decimal field. The internal length of the field relates to the number of digits specified in the precision attribute. Thus if we write

DCL QTY FIXED (5);

This would only require 3 bytes of storage since the five digits are stored as packed decimal in only 3 bytes. Because of this characteristic we must consider how data is stored in the I/O device as well as in main storage when a structure is declared.

If we were to include a field as fixed in the structure such as QTY above, this would reserve only three bytes of storage whereas we may wish to hold a 5-byte zoned decimal numeric field. When the data input is actually packed decimal, such could be the case for tape or disk, then the FIXED attribute may be used successfully in the structure. This attribute then defines the number of digits in the field and, indirectly, the number of bytes.

When the numeric field comes from a device such as a card reader the field cannot be packed decimal on the card, but is considered to be zoned decimal. To read this kind of field, another attribute is needed which will permit the reading of numeric information in zoned format. Zoned numeric information may also be read from tape or disk. This may be done by the use of the PICTURE attribute.

Picture Attribute

The PICTURE attribute is used in a declare statement to define a zoned decimal field. The zoned field may be either character or numeric. In Fig. 9-5 we see the general format for the PICTURE attribute.

DCL *label* PICTURE *'picture-specification';*

Fig. 9-5 *Picture Attribute*

label	A descriptive entry naming the declared variable.
PICTURE	Is a key work identifying a zoned decimal field. May be abbreviated to PIC.
'picture-specification'	This defines the attributes of the field declared. X – defines a character string data field. 9 – defines a zoned decimal numeric field. V – indicates an assumed decimal position. A decimal point does not actually appear in the field but is implied by the V.

Figure 9-6 shows examples of declares using the picture attribute. The first item NAMEA shows a picture containing ten X's. This defines a character string field of ten characters in length. NAMEB defines a field which is equivalent to NAMEA. In this case the repetition factor (10) is used thus indicating that ten of the following picture character X are required. NAMEA and NAMEB could also have been declared as:

DCL (NAMEA,NAMEB) CHAR (10);

or, of course, as:

DCL (NAMEA,NAMEB) PIC '(10)X';

All of these give the same result.

```
DCL   NAMEA   PIC   'XXXXXXXXXX',
      NAMEB   PIC   '(10)X',
      QTY     PIC   '(7)9',
      AMT     PIC   '(5)9V99',
      TØTAL   PIC   '(8)9V99',
      CALC    PIC   'V(5)9',
```

Fig. 9-6

QTY in Fig. 9-6 defines a zoned decimal numeric field consisting of seven numeric digits. The field AMT consists of seven numeric digits of which two are fractional. Internally AMT would consist of seven bytes of storage. On an external device such as a card reader, AMT would require seven columns on the data card. On magnetic devices AMT would require seven positions in the record as zoned decimal information.

TØTAL consists of ten numeric digits, two of which are fractional. CALC consists of five numeric digits, all of which are fractional.

Given a magnetic tape record in the following format:

1–5	Employee Number	Numeric
6–9	Rate (2 decimal)	Numeric
10–15	Net Pay (2 decimal)	Numeric
16–21	Date Hired (Month, Day, Yr.)	Numeric
22–26	Deduction Codes	Numeric

27–30	Unused	
31–50	Name	Character
51–53	Department	Numeric
54–60	Unused	

This record would be declared in PL/I as follows:

```
DCL  1   RECØRD,
         2 NUMBER     PIC '(5)9',
         2 RATE       PIC '99V99',
         2 NET        PIC '(4)9V99',
         2 DATEH,
           3 (MØ,DAY,YR)  PIC '99',
         2 CØDES(5)   PIC '9',
         2 UNUSEDA    PIC '(4)X',
         2 NAME       PIC '(20)X',
         2 DEPT       PIC '999',
         2 UNUSEDB    PIC '(7)X';
```

In RECØRD all fields are declared using picture attributes. Notice that the field CØDES is declared as an array containing five elements. Each element consists of one numeric digit. This approach is used for ease of programming when CØDES is referenced. In some cases it may be preferable to write

2 CØDES PIC '(5)9',

Either method results in the storing of five bytes of data. The method used is entirely the programmer's choice.

Notice that UNUSEDA and UNUSEDB are both declared as character strings. Normally an unused field contains blanks which can only be processed as a character string.

The additional picture characters shown in Fig. 9–7 are normally used for printed output. These characters are used to produce more useful and readable reports for the user. Thus they will usually appear in structures which will ultimately be written onto a printer. Data will normally be assigned to these structures from associated input records. In some cases, of course, data will be calculated internally within the program.

. Inserts a decimal point where written

, Inserts a comma where written

Z Zero suppression

$ Inserts a high order dollar sign or may be used as a floating dollar sign

* Replaces leading zeroes with asterisks

B Inserts a blank where written

CR Prints when field contains a negative value

DB Prints when field contains a negative value

− Prints for negative values

+ Prints for positive values

/ Insertion character

Fig. 9–7 *Additional Picture Characters*

One exception to this is when the Z picture character is used for an input record. In this case the Z acts as a zero insertion character for a numeric field. If the field contains blanks in the high order positions, the Z causes zeroes to be inserted in their place.

Figure 9–8 shows these picture characters used with sample input and output data.

SOURCE DATA	PICTURE SPECIFICATION	RESULTING VALUE
45256.75	'99,999V.99'	45,256.75
00256.75	'ZZ,ZZZV.99'	256.75
00000.75	'ZZ,ZZZV.99'	.75
6800	'$99V.99'	$68.00
0095	'$ZZV.99'	$ .95
0095	'$$$V.99'	$.95
0251	'$$$V.99'	$2.51
0345	'* * *9'	*345
0009	'* * *9'	* * *9
120771	'99B99B99'	12 07 71
005.70	'ZZZV.99CR'	5.70
-005.70	'ZZZV.99CR'	5.70CR

005.70	'ZZZV.99DB'	5.70
-005.70	'ZZZV.99DB'	5.70DB
-005.70	'ZZZV.99-'	5.70-
005.70	'ZZZV.99+'	5.70+

Fig. 9-8 *Use of Picture Characters for Printed Output*

File Declaration

When using the Disk or Tape Operating System, each file used in the PL/I program must be declared. The attributes used in file declaration are shown in Fig. 9-9. The essential characteristics of these attributes have been described on page 69 for use with stream-oriented files. Although there is a similarity to the declaration of record-oriented files, the attributes required vary somewhat depending upon the requirements of the file being used.

The following examples demonstrate how the file attributes are used in PL/I to declare record-oriented files. First we wish to declare a simple card input file. This would be done as follows:

```
DCL CARD FILE RECØRD INPUT
    ENV(MEDIUM(SYSIPT,2501)
    F(80) BUFFERS (2));
```

This declare describes a record-oriented file named CARD. CARD is a name chosen by the programmer which will be used throughout the program to reference the card reader. Notice that this card input comes from the Standard System Input device SYSIPT. SYSIPT is a 2501 card reader. It uses a fixed length unblocked record consisting of 80 bytes in the block. For this file we are using two input buffers which will enhance execution efficiency.

An Optimizer user would declare this file as follows:

```
DCL CARD FILE RECORD INPUT ENV(MEDIUM(SYSIPT,2501)
    F BLKSIZE(80) BUFFERS(2));
```

The next example deals with a disk input file which consists of 100-byte logical records with a blocking factor of 10.

```
DCL FILEA FILE RECORD INPUT ENV(MEDIUM
    (SYS001,2314) F(1000,100) BUFFERS(2));
```

FILE TYPE	SEQUENTIAL							INDEXED				
	INPUT			OUTPUT			UPDATE	SEQUENTIAL			DIRECT	
	CARD	TAPE	DASD	CARD/PRINTER	TAPE	DASD	DASD	INPUT	OUTPUT	UPDATE	INPUT	UPDATE
filename FILE	S D	S D	S D	S D	S D	S D	S D	S D	S D	S D	S D	S D
RECORD	S	S	S	S	S	S	S	S	S	S	S	S
INPUT OUTPUT UPDATE	S	S	S	 S	 S	 S	 S	S	 S	 S	S	 S
SEQUENTIAL DIRECT	D	D	D	D	D	D	D	D	D	D	 S	 S
KEYED								S	S	S	S	S
ENVIRONMENT(MEDIUM(	S S	S S	S S	S S	S S	S S	S S	S S	S S	S S	S S	S S
SYSIPT, SYSPCH, SYSLST, SYSnnn,	C C	C C	C C	 C C C	 C C C	 C C C	 S	 S	 S	 S	 S	 S
2501|2520|2540|1442) 1403|1404|1443|1445) 2400) 2311|2314|3340|2321)	S	 S	 S	C C	 S	 S	 S	 S	 S	 S	 S	 S
U(*maxblocksize*) F(*blocksize*) F(*blocksize, recisize*) V(*maxblocksize*)	 S	C C C C	C C C C	 S	C C C C	C C C C	C C C C	 C C	 C C	 C C	 C C	 C C
BUFFERS(1) BUFFERS(2)	D O	D O	D O	D O	D O	D O	D O					
CTLASA/CTL360				O								
LEAVE NOLABEL NOTAPEMK VERIFY		O O			O O O	 O	 O		 O	 O		 O
CONSECUTIVE INDEXED	D	D	D	D	D	D	D	 S	 S	 S	 S	 S
KEYLENGTH(*n*) EXTENTNUMBER(*n*) INDEXMULTIPLE HIGHINDEX OFLTRACKS(*n*) KEYLOCK(*n*)								S S O O B	S S O O O B	S S O O B	S S O O B	S S O O B
)	S	S	S	S	S	S	S	S	S	S	S	S
EXTERNAL	D	D	D	D	D	D	D	D	D	D	D	D

S — Specify this attribute
D — Default if not specified
O — Optional attribute
C — Choose one of these attributes
B — Specify for blocked files

Fig. 9-9 *Record File Declaration*

In this example FILEA is the name of the extent reserved on the 2314 for the file we are using. SYS001 refers to the physical device upon which FILEA resides. In this case we are dealing with a fixed-length blocked file with a block size of 1000 bytes and a record size of 100 bytes. Notice that the blocking factor is not directly specified but is used to derive the block size. FILEA could be declared for the Optimizer in the following way using a 3340 disk drive:

DCL FILEA RECORD INPUT ENV(MEDIUM(SYS001,3340)
FB BLKSIZE(1000) RECSIZE(100) BUFFERS(2));

The third example shows a printed output file as follows:

DCL REPØRT RECØRD ØUTPUT ENV(MEDIUM(SYSLST,1403)
F(133) BUFFERS(2) CTLASA);

REPØRT is a programmer chosen name which describes the 1403 printer output file. The printer is the Standard System print output called SYSLST. It is a fixed length unblocked file consisting of 133 bytes of data. CTLASA refers to a control character which uses the first byte of output in the logical record. This character is used for printer carriage control for spacing and skipping. Since this character is included, the print line is 133 bytes rather than the 132 bytes which is the length permitted for a 1403 printer. If CTLASA or CTL360 were not used, then this length would be 132 bytes.

When a structure is declared for a print file, it must include all 133 bytes. The control character will be assigned to the first byte of the structure. This one-byte field must be a character string. The character assigned specifies the action to be taken by the printer prior to printing a given line of data. Some commonly used CTLASA characters are shown in Fig. 9-10. For a more complete listing of CTLASA and CTL360 characters, refer to Appendix C.

CODE	USE
blank	Space one line before print
0	Space two lines before print
–	Space three lines before print
+	Suppress spacing
1	Skip to channel one before print

Fig. 9-10

Any of the files previously declared a structure will also be declared to describe the format of the record to be read or written by the program. If the file is blocked or unblocked, this has no effect upon the method of structure declare. Thus in the first example, the card file would have a structure declared consisting of 80 bytes of information. The disk file would have a structure consisting of 100 bytes.

If only part of the logical record is used for data, the structure must still specify the entire record length. Thus if only 60 bytes of data were contained in the data card an additional 20 bytes must be declared to give a total record length of 80. Normally this is done by declaring a character string of 20.

Blocked Records

Magnetic devices such as tape, disk and drum use a method of grouping logical records together into a physical record or block (See Figure 9-11). This causes records to be read and written more efficiently and for the records to use less space on the storage device. When blocking is used in PL/I, only the file declare is affected by it. The size of the block is specified by the number of bytes contained in it. The number of bytes in the logical record is also specified. Notice that the blocking factor is not specified.

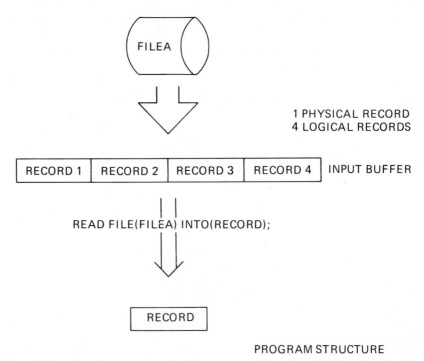

Fig. 9-11

In the rest of the program only logical records are referenced. Therefore the structure in the program will describe the length of a logical record. A READ statement will cause one logical record to be transferred from an input buffer (not declared in PL/I) to the structure.

Output files operate in the reverse. Data is written from an output structure and is transferred to an output buffer where blocking occurs.

Open and Close

The open and close statements used for record-oriented data are no different from those used for stream-oriented statements. Refer to page 73 for the use of these statements.

Read Statement

When using stream oriented files a GET statement was executed to transmit data from the input device to the variables declared in the program. In the case of record oriented files a READ statement is used to transmit data from the file into the structure. Figure 9–12 shows the general format of the READ statement.

---

1 2

READ FILE (*filename*) INTØ (*structure*);

Fig. 9–12

READ	A keyword which must always be specified.
FILE	A keyword which must always be specified.
(*filename*)	The name of the file used in the file declare statement. It is always contained within parentheses.
INTØ	A keyword which must always be specified.
(*structure*)	The level one name of the structure into which data is to be read.

A READ statement is executed each time a data record is required by the program. This causes a logical record to be transferred from the physical device to the structure specified in the READ statement. A READ statement may have a label preceding it, thus permitting branching to the READ statement from elsewhere in the program.

A READ statement for the file CARD, declared formerly, could be written as follows:

READ FILE (CARD) INTØ (WØRK);

In this read, WØRK would be the level-one name of the structure into which the data will be read.

Write Statement

With stream-oriented data, a PUT statement was used to transmit data from the declared variables to the output device. In the case of record files, a WRITE statement is used to transmit data from a structure to the output file. The general format for the WRITE is shown in Fig. 9–13.

---

1 2

WRITE FILE (*filename*) FRØM (*structure*);

Fig. 9–13

WRITE	A keyword which must be specified.
FILE	A keyword which must be specified.
(*filename*)	The name of the file in the file declare statement. Enclosed within parentheses.
FRØM	A keyword which must be specified.
(*structure*)	The level-one name of the structure from which data is to be written.

A WRITE statement for the file named REPØRT, declared previously, would be written as follows:

WRITE FILE (REPØRT) FRØM (PRINT);

In this example data is transferred from the structure called PRINT to the file REPØRT. PRINT would be 133 bytes in length and would contain, as the first byte, the CTLASA control character.

On Endfile

The use of the ENDFILE statement for record files is no different from the use in stream files. Refer to page 75 for a discussion on this statement.

Creating a 3340 Master File

Figure 9-14 shows a program for creating a simple Inventory Master File on a 3340 Direct Access Device from data cards. These cards contain a code in columns 18-19 which identifies the card type. Only codes other than code 10 cards are used to create the master.

```
01  CREATE:PROC OPTIONS(MAIN);
02  DCL CARD RECORD INPUT ENV(MEDIUM(SYSIPT,2501)
        F BLKSIZE(80) BUFFERS(2));
03  DCL 1 CARDREC,
        2 CSTOCK PIC'(10)9',
        2 CLOC,
        3 CROW PIC 'XXX',
        3 CSHELF PIC 'XX',
        3 CBIN PIC 'XX',
        2 CCODE PIC 'XX',
        2 CQTY PIC '(7)9',
        2 CUNIT PIC '(5)9V99',
        2 CDE SC PIC '(17)X',
        2 CUM PIC 'XX',
        2 CFILL PIC '(28)X';
04  DCL FILEA RECORD OUTPUT ENV(MEDIUM(SYS001,3340)
        FB BLKSIZE(500) RECSIZE(50) BUFFERS(2));
05  DCL 1 MREC,
        2 MSTOCK PIC '(10)9',
        2 MLOC,
        3 MROW PIC 'XXX',
        3 MSHELF PIC 'XX',
        3 MBIN PIC 'XX',
        2 MCODE PIC 'XX',
        2 MQTY FIXED(7),
        2 MUNIT FIXED(7,2),
        2 MDESC PIC '(17)X',
        2 MUM PIC 'XX',
        2 MFILL PIC '(4)X';
06  DCL N FIXED(1) INIT(0);
07  OPEN FILE(CARD), FILE(FILEA);
```

```
08  ON ENDFILE (CARD) BEGIN;
09      CLOSE FILE(CARD), FILE(FILEA);
10      STOP;
11      END;

12  READ FILE(CARD) INTO (CARDREC);
13      DO WHILE(N=0);
14          IF CODE = '10' THEN;
                        ELSE DO;
16              MSTOCK=CSTOCK;
17              MLOC=CLOC;
18              MCODE=CCODE;
19              MQTY=CQTY;
20              MUNIT=CUNIT;
21              MDESC=CDESC;
22              MUM=CUM;
23              MFILL=' ';
24              WRITE FILE(FILEA) FROM(MREC);
25              END;
26          READ FILE(CARD) INTO(CARDREC);
27          END;
28  END CREATE;
```

Fig. 9-14 *Creating a Disk File from Data Cards*

All fields in the card input structure are zoned decimal. Some of the fields are numeric and some character string. The master structure is zoned decimal except for Quantity and Unit Cost which are packed (FIXED). Since these structures are not of the same format, each variable is assigned to M_REC individually.

CLØC may be assigned to MLØC since they are both minor structures of the same format. If one had been a minor structure as shown and the other a field with PIC '(7)X', then the assignment could not be made.

Statement 14 is a null THEN clause, that is, a clause with no action. If the code is 10, nothing is to be done and therefore a semicolon terminates the entry. In this case, the ELSE specifies the action to be taken.

Producing a Report from the Inventory Master

Figure 9-15 shows how an Inventory report may be produced from the Master file created in Fig. 9-14. Since the report consists of three different lines of information (see Fig. 9-16) three structures are used for the PRINT file.

The first structure PHEAD1 is used to print the first heading line. Since this line is to appear at the top of a new page the control character in the first print position is a '1'.

The second structure PHEAD2 prints the second heading line. It contains the control character '#' which causes the spacing of one line before this heading is printed.

PDATA is used to print each line of data in the body of the report. The control character '0' causes two lines of spacing.

```
1   REPORT:PROC OPTIONS(MAIN);
2   DCL FILEA RECORD INPUT ENV(MEDIUM(SYS001,3340)
          FB BLKSIZE(500) RECSIZE(50) BUFFERS(2));
3   DCL 1 MREC,
          2 MSTOCK PIC '(10)9',
          2 MLOC,
            3 MROW PIC 'XXX',
            3 MSHELF PIC 'XX',
            3 MBIN PIC 'XX',
          2 MCODE PIC 'XX',
          2 MQTY FIXED(7),
          2 MUNIT FIXED(7,2),
          2 MDESC PIC '(17)X',
          2 MUM PIC 'XX',
          2 MFILL PIC '(4)X';
4   DCL PRINT RECORD OUTPUT ENV(MEDIUM(SYSLST,1403)
          F BLKSIZE(133) BUFFERS(2) CTLASA);
5   DCL 1 PHEAD1,
          2 PHCTL1 PIC '(25)X' INIT('1'),
          2 PHA PIC '(108)X' INIT('INVENTORY MASTER');
6   DCL 1 PHEAD2,
          2 PHCTL 2 PIC'X' INIT(' '),
          2 PHB PIC '(30)X' INIT(' STOCK NUMBER LOCATION'),
          2 PHC PIC '(16)X' INIT('DESCRIPTION'),
          2 PHD PIC '(25)X' INIT ('U M   QUANTITY UNIT COST'),
          2 PHE PIC '(61)X' INIT(' ');
7   DCL 1 PDATA,
          2 PDCTL3 PIC 'XXX' INIT ('0'),
          2 PSTOCK PIC '(10)9',
          2 PFILLA PIC 'XXX' INIT(' '),
          2 PLOC PIC '(12)X',
          2 PDESC PIC '(20)X',
          2 PUM PIC '(5)X',
          2 PQTY PIC '(6)Z9',
          2 PFILLB PIC 'XXX' INIT(' '),
          2 PUNIT PIC '(5)ZV.99',
          2 PFILLC PIC '(62)X' INIT(' ');
```

```
 8  DCL LINELIMIT PIC '99' INIT(60),
           LINECOUNT PIC '99' INIT(0),
           N PIC '9' INIT(0);
 9  OPEN FILE(FILEA), FILE(PRINT);
10  ON ENDFILE(FILEA) BEGIN;
11      CLOSE FILE(FILEA),FILE(PRINT);
12      STOP;
13      END;
14  CALL HEAD;
15  READ FILE(FILEA) INTO(MREC);
16  DO WHILE(N=0);
17      PSTOCK=MSTOCK;
18      PLOC=MROW||'-'||MSHELF||'-'||MBIN;
19      PDESC=MDESC;
20      PUM=MUM;
21      PQTY=MQTY;
22      PUNIT=MUNIT;
23      WRITE FILE(PRINT) FROM(PDATA);
24      LINECOUNT=LINECOUNT+2;
25      IF LINECOUNT>=LINELIMIT THEN CALL HEAD;
26      READ FILE(FILEA) INTO(MREC);
27      END;
28  HEAD:PROC;
29  LINECOUNT=4;
30  WRITE FILE(PRINT) FROM(PHEAD1);
31  WRITE FILE(PRINT) FROM(PHEAD2);
32  END HEAD;
33  END REPORT;
```

Fig. 9-15 *Printing the Master File*

Since a heading is to be printed on each page of output, this activity is included in an internal procedure HEAD. HEAD is called whenever a new page is to be started. LINE_CØUNT is a variable which determines when a given page is filled.

Defined Variable Concepts

As programs become more complex we often face the need to describe a variable in two or more different ways. For instance, to test a field for invalid characters (nonnumeric), the following declare could be used:

DCL FIELD(5) PIC 'X';

```
┌─────────────────────────────────────────────────────────────────────┐
│                        INVENTØRY MASTER                               │
│    STØCK                                                              │
│    NUMBER     LØCATION      DESCRIPTIØN      U_M   QUANTITY UNIT CØST  │
│                                                                       │
│    0087953000 010-05-03 12 V. ALTERNATØR      01       50     26.95   │
│    0200578911 105-10-01 STEREØ FM RADIØ       01      121    269.00   │
│    0200578912 105-10-02 STEREØ TAPE           01       79     89.95   │
│    0200578913 105-10-03 3 SECTIØN ANTENNA     01      576      2.75   │
│    0333000000 099-01-01 WINDSHIELD SEALER     03     1194      0.19   │
└─────────────────────────────────────────────────────────────────────┘
```

Fig. 9-16

This is a five-element array with one character per element. Data contained within it might appear as:

FIELD(5) PIC 'X'

2	3	6	0	1
1	2	3	4	5

Each reference to field would be subscripted and would access only one byte. FIELD(2) would access only the value 3 and FIELD(5) the value 1.

After the field has been tested, we may need to use it as a numeric value. In the example, 23601 may actually represent the dollar value 236.01 which would normally use the picture:

DCL NUM PIC '(3)9V99';

A move of the data from FIELD to NUM would be illegal in most compilers and not really desirable. Instead we use the concept of defining FIELD a second way.

DCL FIELD(5) PIC'X',
    NUM PIC'(3)9V99' DEFINED FIELD;

Now the field has two definitions although the same five bytes of storage are still used. The first byte of NUM is

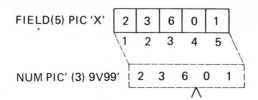

the first element of FIELD. The second byte is the second element and so on. NUM is not a second storage area but simply a redefinition of FIELD.

When the defined concept is used, care must be taken to reference the appropriate field. If the values had been alphanumeric, only FIELD should be referenced.

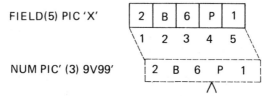

Since FIELD is picture X, nonnumeric characters may be processed legitimately. However if NUM is referenced, in this case, a data exception will occur because nonnumeric characters are invalid for picture 9 fields.

This concept may be extended to structures where several fields need to be redefined. Often a file has several record formats stored in it and we do not know in advance which record is to be read. For example, a file contains the following record formats:

HEADER RECORD

1 - 5	Customer Number
6	Record Identification Code (1)
7 - 25	Customer Name
26 - 50	Customer Address

DETAIL RECORD

1 - 5	Item Code (alphanumeric)
6	Record Identification Code (2)
7 - 9	Quantity

10 - 13	Price
14 - 30	Description

Assuming 50 byte logical records these records may be declared as follows:

```
DCL 1 HEADER,
        2 CUST_NO PIC'(5)9',
        2 CODE     PIC'9',
        2 NAME     PIC'(19)X',
        2 ADDRESS PIC'(25)X';
DCL 1 DETAIL DEF HEADER,
        2 ITEM  PIC'(5)X',
        2 FILL  PIC'X',
        2 QTY   PIC'999',
        2 PRICE PIC'99V99',
        2 DESC  PIC'(17)X';
```

Data would be placed in the structure from a file using a READ into the first structure declared regardless of which format is read. The READ statement might be:

READ FILE(FILEA) INTO(HEADER);

In PL/I, the second structure does not need to be as long as the structure it defines, but it may not exceed the original length. If a field in the second structure is the same as the first, it must still be specified to account for the number of bytes occupied. The only exception is when this field is the last in the structure. In this case it may be omitted from the second structure. HEADER and DETAIL may be portrayed as follows:

When a code 1 is read, only fields in the first structure are referenced since this code contains a customer number, name, and address. Any reference to item, quantity, price, or description would be invalid since the pictures do not correspond to data in the structure.

A code 2 is shown in the next example:

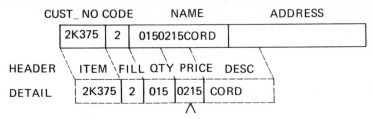

In this case it only makes sense to reference the names in DETAIL. That is item, quantity, price, and description are the fields in this format and they contain the valid pictures for this data. The only exception to this is CODE since it is already described correctly in the first structure. It is unnecessary to refer to FILL.

Reports Using Defined Structures

The PRINT file used in Fig. 9–15 required the use of three structures. Each of these structures consisted of 133 bytes for a total of 399 bytes. Since the program requires the use of only one structure at any given time, it would be more efficient if two of these structures could be eliminated, thus saving 266 bytes.

The Defined attribute permits the use of one area of storage which can be referenced as though several areas were reserved. The structure used by the programmer depends upon the data requirements at any given time. Defined structures cannot use the INITIAL attribute, thus all data must be assigned or, in the case of the READ, placed in the structure by the input action.

The original structure upon which other structures are defined must specify the exact length of the record. Subsequent structures are defined upon the original structure. They may be less than or equal in length to the original structure, but not longer. All I/O operations refer to the original structure.

Fig. 9–17 shows an alternate solution to the REPØRT program using Defined structures for the print file.

```
01   ALT :PROC OPTIONS(MAIN);
02   DCL FILEA RECORD INPUT ENV(MEDIUM(SYS001,3340)
           FB BLKSIZE(500) RECSIZE(50) BUFFERS(2));
03   DCL 1 MREC,
             2 MSTOCK PIC '(10)9',
             2 MLOC,
               3 MROW PIC 'XXX',
               3 MSHELF PIC 'XX',
```

```
            3 MBIN PIC 'XX',
         2 MCODE PIC 'XX',
         2 MQTY FIXED(7),
         2 MUNIT FIXED(7,2),
         2 MDESC PIC '(17)X',
         2 MUM PIC 'XX',
         2 MFILL PIC '(4)X';
04  DCL PRINT RECORD OUTPUT ENV(MEDIUM(SYSLST,1403)
        F BLKSIZE(133) BUFFERS(2) CTLASA);
05  DCL 1 PHEAD1,
         2 PHCTL1 PIC '(25)X',
         2 PHA PIC '(108)X';
06  DCL 1 PHEAD2 DEF PHEAD1,
         2 PHCTL2 PIC 'X',
         2 PHB PIC '(30)X',
         2 PHC PIC '(16)X',
         2 PHD PIC '(25)X',
         2 PHE PIC '(61)X';
07  DCL 1 PDATA DEF PHEAD1,
         2 PDCTL3 PIC 'XXX',
         2 PSTOCK PIC '(10)9',
         2 PFILLA PIC 'XXX',
         2 PLOC PIC '(12)X',
         2 PDESC PIC '(20)X',
         2 PUM PIC '(5)X',
         2 PQTY PIC '(6)Z9',
         2 PFILLB PIC 'XXX',
         2 PUNIT PIC '(5)ZV.99',
         2 PFILLC PIC '(62)X' ;
08  DCL CLEAR PIC '(133)X' DEF PHEAD1;
09  DCL LINELIMIT PIC '99' INIT(60),
        LINECOUNT PIC '99' INIT(0),
        N PIC '9' INIT(0);
10  OPEN FILE(FILEA), FILE(PRINT);
11  ON ENDFILE(FILEA) BEGIN;
12     CLOSE FILE(FILEA),FILE(PRINT);
13     STOP;
14     END;
15  CALL HEAD;
16  READ FILE(FILEA) INTO(MREC);
17  DO WHILE(N=0);
18     CLEAR='0';   /* SET CTLASA TO 0 AND DATA LINE TO SPACES */
19     PSTOCK=MSTOCK;
20     PLOC=MROW||'-'||MSHELF||'-'||MBIN;
```

```
21      PDESC=MDESC;
22      PUM=MUM;
23      PQTY=MQTY;
24      PUNIT=MUNIT;
25      WRITE FILE(PRINT) FROM(PHEAD1);
26      LINECOUNT=LINECOUNT+2;
27      IF LINECOUNT>=LINELIMIT THEN CALL HEAD;
28      READ FILE(FILEA) INTO(MREC);
29      END;
30  HEAD:PROC;
31  LINECOUNT=4;
32  CLEAR='1';
33  PHA='INVENTORY MASTER';
34  WRITE FILE(PRINT) FROM(PHEAD1);
35  CLEAR=' ';
36  PHB=' STOCK NUMBER LOCATION';
37  PHC='DESCRIPTION';
38  PHD='U M QUANTITY UNIT COST';
39  WRITE FILE(PRINT) FROM(PHEAD1);
40  END HEAD;
41  END ALT;
```

Fig. 9-17 *Alternate to Report Program Using Defined Structures*

The first structure PHEAD1 consists of 133 bytes and represents the format of the first heading. Subsequent structures define a different way of representing the same 133 bytes depending upon the requirements of the line to be printed. A fourth variable, CLEAR, is used to clear the entire area of data left over from previous operations.

All WRITEs refer to the first structure declared regardless of which structure received the data. In HEAD, each heading line is produced by assigning the appropriate CTLASA character to CLEAR. This serves a two-fold function. First, the control character is placed in the first byte of the field. Then, since the literal assigned is shorter in length than CLEAR, blank characters are assigned to the remainder of the field. This ensures no garbage remains from any previous use of any of the defined structures.

Now the appropriate data is moved to the structure to create the desired line. For instance, statement 33 assigns the literal for the main heading to PHA. Similarly the second line of the heading is set up in statements 35 to 38.

Balance Line Method

Figure 9-18 shows top-down development of a generally accepted method for sequentially updating a master file with input transactions. The minimum configuration consists of an input master file, an input transaction file, and an output master file which has been updated. A printer is commonly used for error messages.

1. Open files

2. Read Master

3. Read Card

4. Do While there are input records

> 4.1   If Master < Card Then Lowtag = Master
> > Else Lowtag = Card

> 4.2   If Lowtag = nines Then Close files
> > Stop

> 4.3   If Master = Lowtag Then MSW = 1
> > Move Master to Output area
> > Read Master

> 4.4   Do While Card = Lowtag

> > 4.4.1   If Card is 'new' Then
> > > If Output = Card Then Print error
> > > > Else Move Card to Output area
> > > > MSW = 1
> > > Else

> > 4.4.2   If Card is 'revise' Then
> > > If Output not = Card Then Print error
> > > > Else revise output master
> > > Else

> > 4.4.3   If Card is 'delete' Then
> > > If Output not = Card Then Print error
> > > Else DSW = 1

> > 4.4.4   Read Card

> 4.5   If MSW = 1 Then MSW = 0
> > If DSW = 1 Then DSW = 0
> > > Else Write Updated Master from
> > > Output area

Fig. 9-18 *Top Down Balance Line*

LØWTAG is a technique used to identify the input file with the lowest control field. If sequencing of the file was by account number, then LØWTAG would become the account of either the master or transaction file depending upon which was lowest. Each record is then compared against LØWTAG to determine the type of updating which can be done.

Master accounts to be updated are processed in the output structure. When a new master record is to be created the output structure is also used with the existing master record remaining in the input structure.

Figure 9-19 shows a program based on the BALANCE LINE UPDATING METHØD. It is an inventory application consisting of input and output masters on 3340 DASD's and a card transaction file.

The program begins by reading a Master(FILEA) and a Transaction (CARD). The lowest Stock number from these two files is assigned to a variable called LOWTAG. This variable is used for comparison purposes throughout the program. When both inputs reach end of file, LOWTAG will become 9's and the job is terminated.

In statement 21 the master is compared to LOWTAG. If it is equal, the master record is moved to the output area where all updating will occur. To show that this has been done, MSW is set to 1.

Statements 26 to 53 process transactions against the master in the output area. This continues while the card is equal to LOWTAG. A card code of 01 indicates a new master is to be created. In this case the output master must not be equal to the card. A new master is then created in the output area.

Codes 20 and 30 are revisions to an existing master. In this case the card must be equal to the master and the appropriate revision is made.

Code 40 is a delete. If an equal master exists, DSW is turned on to indicate a delete. Notice that in every case when a transaction is processed, the updated master has not been written, nor has a new master been read during this time. This procedure allows for multiple updates against the existing master.

When CSTOCK becomes greater than LOWTAG, processing continues at statement 54. Here the updated master is written on FILEB unless DSW is on. In this case, no write is executed and the record is deleted from the output file.

Internal procedures READM and READC are used to read a master and card transaction respectively. Each of these procedures tests for end of file and assigns 9's to the appropriate stock number when the end is reached. Each file is also tested for ascending sequence of the stock number. Since this is a sequential update, it is essential that all records are sequenced correctly. A sequence error causes the program to terminate.

```
1   UPDATE :PROC OPTIONS(MAIN);
2   DCL FILEA RECORD INPUT ENV (MEDIUM(SYS001,3340)
          FB BLKSIZE(500) RECSIZE(50) BUFFERS(2));
3   DCL 1 MREC,
          2 MSTOCK PIC '(10)9',
          2 MLOC,
```

```
                  3 MROW PIC 'XXX',
                  3 MSHELF PIC 'XX',
                  3 MBIN PIC 'XX',
               2 MCODE PIC 'XX',
               2 MQTY FIXED(7),
               2 MUNIT FIXED(7,2),
               2 MDESC PIC '(17)X',
               2 MUM PIC 'XX',
               2 MFILL PIC '(4)X';
 4  DCL CARD RECORD INPUT ENV(MEDIUM(SYSIPT,2501)
        F BLKSIZE(80) BUFFERS(2));
 5  DCL 1 CARDREC,
               2 CSTOCK PIC'(10)9',
               2 CLOC,
                  3 CROW PIC 'XXX',
                  3 CSHELF PIC 'XX',
                  3 CBIN PIC 'XX',
               2 CCODE PIC 'XX',
               2 CQTY PIC '(7)9',
               2 CUNIT PIC '(5)9V99',
               2 CDESC PIC '(17)X',
               2 CUM PIC 'XX',
               2 CFILL PIC '(28)X';
 6  DCL FILEB RECORD OUTPUT ENV(MEDIUM(SYS001,3340)
        FB BLKSIZE(500) RECSIZE(50) BUFFERS(2));
 7  DCL 1 UREC,
               2 USTOCK PIC '(10)9',
               2 ULOC,
                  3 UROW PIC 'XXX',
                  3 USHELF PIC 'XX',
                  3 UBIN PIC 'XX',
               2 UCODE PIC 'XX',
               2 UQTY FIXED(7),
               2 UUNIT FIXED(7,2),
               2 UDESC PIC '(17)X',
               2 UUM PIC 'XX',
               2 UFILL PIC '(4)X';
 8  DCL LOWTAG PIC'(10)9',
           PMSTOCK PIC '(10)9' INIT(0),
           PCSTOCK PIC '(10)9' INIT(0),
           MSW FIXED (1) INIT(0),
           DSW FIXED (1) INIT(0);
 9  OPEN FILE (FILEA), FILE(FILEB), FILE(CARD);
10  USTOCK = 0;    /* IN CASE THE FIRST CARD IS AN ADD */
```

```
11   CALL READM;
12   CALL READC;
13   DO WHILE('1'B);
14       IF MSTOCK < CSTOCK THEN LOWTAG = MSTOCK;
                                ELSE LOWTAG = CSTOCK;
16       IF LOWTAG = 9999999999 THEN DO;    /* END OF JOB */
17           PUT SKIP LIST('END OF UPDATE');
18           CLOSE FILE (FILEA), FILE(FILEB), FILE(CARD);
19           STOP;
20           END;
21       IF MSTOCK = LOWTAG THEN DO;
22           MSW = 1;
23           UREC = MREC;      /* MOVE INPUT MASTER TO OUTPUT */
24           CALL READM;
25           END;
26       DO WHILE (CSTOCK = LOWTAG);
27           IF CCODE = '01' THEN DO;      /* NEW */
28               IF CSTOCK = USTOCK THEN CALL ERROR;
                 /* ALREADY ON MASTER */
29                 ELSE DO;
30                     USTOCK=CSTOCK;      /* CREATE NEW MASTER */
31                     ULOC=CLOC;
32                     UCODE=' ';
33                     UQTY=CQTY;
34                     UUNIT=CUNIT;
35                     UDESC=CDESC;
36                     UUM=CUM;
37                     UFILL=' ';
38                     MSW=1;    /* MASTER IN OUTPUT AREA */
39                     END;
40               END;
41           ELSE IF CCODE = '20' | CCODE = '30' THEN DO; /* REVISE */
42                   IF CSTOCK ¬ = USTOCK THEN CALL ERROR;
                     /* NO EQUAL MAST */
43                     ELSE DO;
44                         IF CCODE = '20' THEN UQTY=UQTY+CQTY;
45                                         ELSE UQTY=UQTY-CQTY;
46                         END;
47                   END;
48           ELSE IF CCODE = '40' THEN DO;    /* DELETE */
49                   IF CSTOCK ¬ = USTOCK THEN CALL ERROR;
                     /* NO EQUAL MAST */
50                     ELSE DSW = 1;
51                   END;
52           CALL READC;
```

```
53      END;
                    /* * * CSTOCK > LOWTAG * * */
54      IF MSW = 1 THEN DO;
55          MSW = 0;
56             IF DSW = 1 THEN DSW = 0;
57                 ELSE WRITE FILE(FILEB) FROM(UREC);
58             END;
59  END;      /* END OF MAIN-LINE LOGIC */
60  READM:PROC;   /* READ AND SEQUENCE CHECK MASTER */
61  ON ENDFILE(FILEA) MSTOCK=9999999999;
62  READ FILE(FILEA) INTO(MREC);
63  IF MSTOCK <= PMSTOCK THEN DO;
64      PUT SKIP LIST ('MASTER FILE SEQUENCE ERROR AT',MSTOCK);
65      CALL TERMINATE;
66      END;
67  PMSTOCK=MSTOCK;
68  END READM;
69  READC:PROC;     /* READ AND SEQUENCE CHECK TRANSACTION */
70  ON ENDFILE(CARD) CSTOCK=9999999999;
71  READ FILE(CARD) INTO(CARDREC);
72  IF CSTOCK < PCSTOCK THEN DO;
73      PUT SKIP LIST('TRANSACTION FILE SEQUENCE ERROR AT',
           CSTOCK);
74      CALL TERMINATE;
75      END;
76  PCSTOCK=CSTOCK;
77  END READC;
78  ERROR:PROC;
79  PUT SKIP LIST('ERROR IN UPDATE WITH TRANSACTION',CSTOCK);
80  PUT LIST('UPDATE CODE IS',CCODE);
81  END ERROR;
82  TERMINATE:PROC;
83  CLOSE FILE(FILEA),FILE(FILEB),FILE(CARD);
84  STOP;
85  END TERMINATE;
86  END UPDATE;
```

Fig. 9-19

Qualification

When structures are used, it is possible to have the same variable name appear in each structure. This can result from the use of the LIKE attribute or simply as a matter of the programmer's choice. Thus we may have structures as follows:

```
DCL 1 INPUT,
      2 NUM PIC '(5)9',
      2 NAME PIC '(20)X',
      2 AMT PIC '(4)9V99',
      2 CODE PIC 'X',
      2 DATE,
        3 (MO,DAY,YEAR) PIC '99';
DCL 1 OUTPUT,
      2 NUM PIC '(5)9',
      2 NAME PIC '(20)X',
      2 AMT PIC '(4)9V99',
      2 DATE,
        3 (MO,DAY,YEAR) PIC '99';
```

The problem which now appears is what happens when we refer to a field like NUM. Which NUM are we referencing since there are two different NUMs? To refer to NUM in INPUT we write INPUT.NUM. This qualifies NUM and says it is the field in INPUT we are referring to. Other fields would be referenced as follows:

```
INPUT.NAME
OUTPUT.NAME
OUTPUT.DATE.DAY
```

Since CODE does not appear in both structures, it does not need to be qualified.

By Name

When structures such as INPUT and OUTPUT are used data may be assigned easily from one to the other by means of the BY NAME attribute. This is done as follows:

```
OUTPUT = INPUT, BY NAME;
```

Each field from INPUT will be assigned to OUTPUT with the exception of CODE. CODE is not assigned since its name is not found in the output structure. All other names are found in both structures and therefore the data is transferred for them.

Like

If we have a need for two identical structures, this can be accomplished without the monotony of declaring each item a second time. This may be done using the LIKE attribute:

```
DCL 1 ORDER,
        2 INVOICE PIC '(7)9',
        2 CUST_NO PIC '(5)9',
        2 NAME PIC '(15)X',
        2 ADR_LINE_1 PIC '(20)X',
        2 ADR_LINE_2 PIC '(20)X',
        2 ITEM PIC '(5)X',
        2 AMOUNT PIC '(4)9V99';
    DCL 1 PROCESS LIKE ORDER;
```

This is equivalent to declaring PROCESS with each entry shown in OR-DER. Each name in PROCESS may be referred to as though it had been individually declared. These names may be referenced using qualification or with the BY NAME attribute as discussed previously.

Position

The POSITION attribute is used with the DEFINED statement to permit the defining of a portion of a variable or structure. This attribute specifies the starting byte used for a new definition of the field.

```
    DCL PART_CODE PIC '(10)X',
        MODEL PIC'(5)9' DEF PART_CODE POSITION(3);
```

In this declare, if PART_CODE contained A237890BLW the declare for MODEL would access the value 37890 which is a 5 byte numeric field beginning in position 3 of PART_CODE.

Defined structures may also use POSITION as shown in the following example:

```
DCL 1 MASTER,
        2 CODE PIC 'X',
        2 CUST_NUM PIC '(6)9',
        2 NAME PIC '(13)X',
        2 ADDR PIC '(15)X',
        2 BALANCE PIC '(5)9V99';
```

```
DCL 1 DETAIL DEF MASTER POSITION(8),
       2 ITEM PIC '(7)X',
       2 DESC PIC '(25)X',
       2 QTY PIC '(4)9',
       2 AMOUNT PIC '(4)9V99';
```

In this case the second format begins with the same two fields CODE and CUST_NUM. Since these have already been declared in the first structure, there is no need to declare them again in the defined structure. Thus DETAIL begins at position 8 of MASTER and describes only those fields which are different from the first format.

Based Structures

Structures used with record-oriented files occupy the storage area reserved via the declare. In addition to this area, the buffers specified in the file declare also occupy storage. The number of bytes for the buffer(s) relates directly to the block size and whether 1 or 2 buffers are used. Figure 9-20 shows this relationship.

BUFFER 1 [   ]

BUFFER 2 [   ]

STRUCTURE [   ]

Fig. 9-20

As each READ statement is executed, a logical record is transferred from a buffer to the structure. As your program is processing the record in the structure, IOCS (Input/Output Control System) brings another record into the buffer from the input device. The reverse is true for output files.

This creates two areas of inefficiency. The first is the time involved in the transfer of data from the buffer to the structure. Although this time is minimal per record, it adds up to considerable time lost when thousands of records are processed.

The second area of inefficiency relates to the usage of storage. The use of based structures permits the organization of the structure to be located in the buffer itself. Figure 9-21 shows how this is accomplished.

```
DCL PTR PØINTER;
DCL 1 RECØRD BASED (PTR),
        2-------,
        2-------,
        2-------,
        2-------;
READ FILE (CARD) SET (PTR);
```

Fig. 9-21

The structure RECØRD is declared in the usual manner except that the level-one entry is based on a pointer PTR. This pointer is declared separately and is set in the READ statement. The record is made available in the buffer since the pointer is set to the address of the buffer. Thus the structure itself does not require additional storage.

If the data records for a given file have several formats, additional structures are declared, each based on the same pointer. When several files are used, each file requires a separate pointer and thus separate structures.

Locate Statement

Output files may be created using records based on pointers. The major difference between input and output is the necessity to move data to the structure before the output operation occurs. Thus the pointer must be set to the output buffer before data can be moved to the buffer. Figure 9-22 demonstrates this method.

```
DCL A PØINTER;
DCL 1 PRINT BASED(A),
        2------,
        2------,
        2------,
        2------;
DO WHILE(N=0);
READ FILE (CARD) SET (PTR);
LØCATE PRINT FILE (ØUT) SET (A);
/* ASSIGN DATA TØ THE ØUTPUT STRUCTURE */
END;
```

Fig. 9-22

In this example LØCATE sets the pointer A to the output buffer prior to assigning data to structure PRINT. No WRITE statement is executed. When the LØCATE is executed the next time the previous record in the buffer is automatically written. The last record is written when the file is closed.

ADDR Function

The ADDR (address) built-in function is used to supply a storage address to a pointer variable. A variable based on this pointer will then take on the address of the pointer. Figure 9-23 shows an array TABLE with 100 elements each containing 22 bytes of data. Each element contains three different items of information. If I contained the value three as a subscript for TABLE, then the statement

$$P = ADDR(TABLE(I));$$

causes the address of the third element of the array to be stored in the pointer P. Since the structure DATA is based on P, it now references the bytes in element 3 of TABLE. This data may now be manipulated like any other data without the use of subscripting the variable names.

```
DCL TABLE(100) PIC '(22)X',
    P POINTER,
    1 DATA BASED(P),
    2 ACT PIC '(5)9',
    2 DESC PIC '(10)X',
    2 AMT PIC '(5)9V99';
        .
        .
        .

P = ADDR(TABLE(I));
        .
        .
        .

AMT = AMT + IN_AMT;
```

Fig. 9-23

Programming Problems

1. An automobile manufacturer maintains a sequential 2400-tape file showing the number of vehicles presently in their shipping yard. This information is recorded for each make within each model. The master file (blocked 10) is as follows:

1- 3	Make
4- 5	Model
6-10	Number of vehicles in shipping

Card transactions are in this format:

1-3	Make
4-5	Model
6	Code 1 - Going into shipping (add)
	2 - Leaving shipping (subtract)

Write a program to update the existing master file using the card transactions. The updating process should create a new master file and print a report showing the latest status of the updated master. No new records are to be added to the file nor are any records to be deleted.

2. A bank maintains a 2314 disk file for all its customers with savings accounts. The master file is an unblocked sequential file in the following format:

1- 6	Account Number
7-12	Date of Last Update
13-19	Present Balance
20-26	Balance at Last Month's End
27-40	Customer's Name
41-60	Customer's Address

Updating transactions are on cards in the following formats:

1- 6	Account Number	
7-12	Date	
13-19	Amount	
80	Code	2 - Deposit
		3 - Withdrawal
		4 - Closing Account

A code 1 in column 80 may also be used for opening a new account. In this case the transaction has the same format as the master.

An update program using the Balance Line Method is to be written considering the following statements:

1. There may be more than one transaction per master record.

2. An overdraft is unacceptable. If this occurs print an appropriate error message but do not terminate the program.

3. All master records will not necessarily receive updating.

4. A new account may be followed by one or more deposits.

5. All transactions for a given account will be in sequence by the code in column 80.

3. A data processing consultant maintains a library of books, publications, and articles relating to the profession. A record of these by title is stored on a disk file in 60 byte records. Some of these records are as follows:

> An Introduction to Computer Languages
> Computers and Society
> Concepts of Data Base

A KWIC (keyword in context) index listing is required of these titles for easy reference in the organization. A keyword is one which is not an article such as *a, an, to,* or *of.* Each title is listed once for each keyword in alphabetical order. A title containing 3 keywords will appear three times in the list. The titles above would be listed as follows:

Concepts of Data	Base
An Introduction to	Computer Languages
	Computers and Society
	Concepts of Data Base
Concepts of	Data Base
An	Introduction to Computer Languages
An Introduction to Computer	Languages
Computers and	Society
	Keyword column

4. The file described in problem 3 is to be revised to improve its usefulness and flexibility. You have been assigned the task of redesigning the file to allow for the addition of author and publisher to the record. In addition, provision is to be made for updating the file. This should provide for adding new records and deleting records from the file. Redesign the record format and write the update program.

5. A trucking firm wishes to depreciate a tractor purchased for $36,000 over a period of 5 years. Using the straight-line method, show the book value, annual depreciation, and cumulative depreciation over the years. Assume a trade-in value of $9,000 at the end of this time. Output should appear as follows:

Year	Book Value	Annual Depreciation	Cumulative Depreciation
0	36,000	0	0
1	30,600	5,400	5,400
2	25,200	5,400	10,800
3	19,800	5,400	16,200
4	14,400	5,400	21,600
5	9,000	5,400	27,000

6. The declining balance method of depreciation uses a constant percentage to compute the depreciation each year. Each year's depreciation is found by multiplying the current book value by the percentage. Using 40%, produce the above table with the declining balance method.

7. Time cards are prepared for each employee showing the number of hours worked for each day of the week. The following format is used.

1 - 20	Name
21 - 22	Monday Hours
23 - 24	Tuesday ''
25 - 26	Wednesday ''
27 - 28	Thursday ''
29 - 30	Friday ''
31 - 34	Rate per hour

Produce the following report after calculating the total hours and gross salary. Print a total for all employees at the end. Note: An array may be used as an element of a structure.

JOHNSON SPECIALTIES
PAYROLL
                    HOURS WORKED

NAME	MON	TUES	WED	THURS	FRI	TOTAL HOURS	RATE	GROSS SALARY
JONES S	8	9	7	8	8	40	3.20	128.00
KEAN M	8	8	10	10	8	44	3.00	132.00
MAN J	7	0	8	9	8	32	·4.00	128.00

                                              TOTAL GROSS   388.00

8. Produce a bank statement from the following record formats. The first record supplies the balance forward and account information. Subsequent records contain only one transaction: either a check or a deposit.

	Format 1
1 – 3	Branch
4 – 7	Account No.
8 – 13	Period Ending Date (DDMM)
14 – 33	Customer Name
34 – 53	Customer Address Line 1
54 – 73	Customer Address Line 2
74 – 80	Balance Forward

	Format 2
1 – 3	Branch
4 – 7	Account No.
8	Code – 1 – Check
	2 – Deposit
9 – 14	Amount
15 – 18	Date

The statement allows up to three checks and one deposit on a given date. These should be printed on the same line. Output should appear as follows:

Atlantic National Bank   Account No.
Account Statement   237 2810

Jones Mfg. Co Ltd   Period Ending   Balance
Westway Drive   23-10-77   Forward
Sydney Nova Scotia   127.50

Checks	Checks	Checks	Deposits	Date	Balance
15.00				01/10	112.50
7.50	2.85			03/10	102.15
12.00	7.98	57.12	75.00	07/10	100.05
17.05				07/10	83.00
77.00	32.50			10/10	-26.50
			275.56	15/10	249.06
10.17	175.35			19/10	63.54
9.10				23/10	54.44

10

Indexed Sequential

In Chapter 9 the use of sequential, record-oriented files was discussed. Another form of a record type file is called INDEXED SEQUENTIAL. This type of data organization is restricted to direct access devices such as disks or data cells.

The term indexed sequential refers to the method used for organizing the data. All records are stored in the DASD (Direct Access Storage Device) in a sequential manner. The sequence is determined by a key which is specified by the programmer. A key refers to a field in each record such as a part number, payroll number, or customer number, etc. The actual key used, of course, depends upon the application.

Since the records are in sequence by the key, access of the file may be sequential. Each record is unique and thus each key must be unique. No duplication (equal keys) is allowed.

The indexed sequential file also includes, in addition to the data, a series of indexes. These indexes are used to permit the program to access each record in the file directly. That is, if we wished to read a record containing a key of 237010, this record could be read directly without the necessity of reading other records in the file.

Indexed Sequential File Declaration

Figure 9-9 shows the attributes to be used when declaring an Indexed Sequential file for the D- compiler or the PL/I Optimizer. Notice that the indexed sequential section is divided into two sections. The first defines the attributes to be used when the file is to be processed sequentially. The second section is used when the file is to be directly accessed.

The attributes for indexed sequential are selected in the same way as for sequential file organization. However, some of the attributes which relate to indexed sequential may require a separate explanation.

KEYLENGTH(n)	Indicates the number of bytes in the key field for each record. A 7-character part number would use KEYLENGTH(7) as an attribute.
EXTENTNUMBER(n)	Indicates the number of extents used to create the particular file being accessed. A discussion of extents is beyond the scope of this book. Your computer center should be able to supply the information needed for this attribute.
INDEXMULTIPLE and HIGHINDEX	Normally used only for very large files. For student use they are rarely specified.
ØFLTRACKS(n)	Specifies the number of tracks per cylinder reserved for overflow data. This is used when new records are being added to the file.
KEYLØC(n)	Used whenever logical records are blocked on an indexed sequential file. When this is done n refers to the relative location of the key within the block. If the key is in positions 1–7 of the block this attribute would be KEYLØC(1).

The following pages contain sample programs for using indexed sequential files. Refer to these programs for sample file declare statements.

Creating an Indexed Sequential File

The first step in using indexed sequential is to create a file to work with. This requires some additional statements. A special WRITE format is used for creating indexed sequential files. The general format is shown in Fig. 10-1.

```
1 2

  WRITE FILE(filename) FRØM(structure)
       KEYFRØM(expression);
```

Fig. 10-1

This WRITE is similar to the WRITE statement used for sequential files except for the addition of the KEYFRØM(*expression*). The key used for the record to be written is taken from the expression. The expression must always evaluate to a character string. This could be a variable name as follows:

WRITE FILE(MASTER) FRØM(ØUT) KEYFRØM(ACCØUNT);

In this example ACCØUNT must be a character string variable declare with either the CHARACTER(/) or PICTURE X attribute. Another use could be an expression such as

WRITE FILE(MASTER) FRØM(ØUT) KEYFRØM(A||B);

This creates a key by taking the result of the concatenation of A and B.

Finally a literal character string could be used in the KEYFRØM as follows:

WRITE FILE(MASTER) FRØM(ØUT) KEYFRØM('00000');

This uses a key consisting of a character string of five zeroes. These zeroes would be in zoned decimal representation.

Another useful statement for indexed sequential is the ØN KEY condition. Its general format is shown in Fig. 10-2.

```
1 2

  ØN KEY(filename) action;
```

Fig. 10-2

The ØN KEY functions in a manner similar to the ØN ENDFILE discussed in Chap. 5. It relates only to the file specified in the statement. The action will be taken when a Key Error occurs for that file. A Key Error may be detected for several reasons.

1. A duplicate key is found for this file.

2. A sequence error is present in the file.

3. When the file is being directly accessed and an equal key is not found, a key error will be the result.

4. Whenever the file is filled to capacity and cannot accept another record, a key error will occur.

Used properly, as we shall see in following programs, the KEY condition may be used to the benefit of the programmer. It allows the program to retain control when an error occurs. Without ∅N KEY, a key error returns control to the supervisor program thus terminating further execution by our program. On many occasions this is not desirable.

The ∅N KEY statement may be used in a manner similar to the ∅N END-FILE. Thus it may contain a single statement to be executed or, if several are required, a BEGIN block may be used. An example of the ∅N KEY is as follows:

```
ON KEY(FILEH) BEGIN;
    PUT SKIP LIST('KEY ERROR IN',WORK);
    SUM=SUM+1;
    END;
```

Here a BEGIN block is used which contains several actions. If a key error occurs during an input or output operation, control is transferred to this block. A message is printed and one is added to the counter SUM. Control then is passed to the statement which follows the input or output command which created the key error.

Creating an Indexed Subscription File

We are now ready to create an indexed sequential file. Suppose we wish to create a file of magazine subscribers so that the file may be updated directly or read sequentially as required.

Let's assume that the data is presently available on magnetic tape in the following format:

1-4	Subscription Number
5	Record Code
6-24	Name of Subscriber
25-44	Address of Subscriber
45-50	Date of Final Issue

We want to read records from this tape file and create an indexed file using the Subscription Number as a key. In addition, a dummy first record is desired with a key of 0000. A maximum of 10 key errors are permitted but if errors exceed this limit the run should be terminated. The following is a top down development of the solution.

MAKE – Top Down Development

1. Open Files

2. Create first dummy record

3. Load FILEH from DATA File

4. Close Files

5. Stop

(Step 3 which is responsible for loading FILEH is further developed into lower level components.)

3. LOAD

   3.1 Read initial data record

   3.2 Repeat level 3.2 until end of file

      3.2.1 On key error print message

      add 1 to Sum

      3.2.2 Write record on FILEH

      3.2.3 If Sum exceeds 10 print message

      terminate the job

      3.2.4 Read data

Figure 10-3 shows the program for MAKE. The top level consists of statements 5 to 10. Step 3 is developed into an internal procedure called LOAD.

```
01  MAKE:PROC OPTIONS(MAIN);
02  DCL DATA RECORD INPUT ENV(MEDIUM(SYS001,2400)F
          BLKSIZE(50) BUFFERS(2)),
          FILEH RECORD OUTPUT KEYED ENV(MEDIUM(SYS000,3340) F
              BLKSIZE(50) INDEXED KEYLENGTH(4)
              EXTENTNUMBER(3) OFLTRACKS(1));
03  DCL SUM FIXED(2) INIT(0),
          1 RECORD,
```

```
             2 SUBSCRIBER PIC'(4)X',
             2 CODE PIC'9',
             2 NAME PIC' (19)X',
             2 ADDRESS PIC' (20)X',
             2 DATE PIC' (6)9';
04  DCL WORK PIC'(50)X' DEF RECORD;
05  I=0;        /* END OF FILE SWITCH */
06  OPEN FILE(DATA), FILE(FILEH);
07  WRITE FILE(FILEH) FROM(RECORD) KEYFROM('0000');
08  CALL LOAD;
09  CLOSE FILE(DATA), FILE(FILEH);
10  STOP;
11  LOAD: PROC;
                   /* LOAD TAPE RECORDS ONTO IS FILE */
12  ON ENDFILE(DATA) I=1;
13  READ FILE(DATA) INTO(RECORD);
14  DO WHILE(I=0);
15     ON KEY(FILEH) BEGIN;
16        PUT SKIP LIST('KEY ERROR IN',WORK);
17        SUM=SUM+1;
18        END;
19     WRITE FILE(FILEH) FROM(RECORD) KEYFROM(SUBSCRIBER);
20     IF SUM>10 THEN DO;
21        PUT SKIP LIST('ERRORS EXCEED LIMIT-JOB TERMINATED');
22        I=1;    /* FORCES END OF DO */
23        END;
24     READ FILE(DATA) INTO(RECORD);
25     END;
26  END LOAD;
27  END MAKE;
```

Fig. 10-3

LOAD begins by establishing the end of file action for the tape file DATA. This consists of setting I to 1 which will terminate the DO WHILE when end of file is reached. Next, the initial read for file DATA brings the input data into RECORD. The key condition in the DO WHILE prints the error message and a copy of the record which created the error. One is added to SUM as a tally of this error. The ON KEY could have been outside of the DO with no essential change in the logic.

The record is written in statement 19 using SUBSCRIBER as the key. If a key error does not occur, processing continues at statement 20. If an error did occur, control passes to statements 15 through 18. When the Begin block is finished, control then passes back to statement 20 and processing continues.

When the number of errors exceeds 10 statements, 20 to 23 will print another error message and the program will be terminated. Otherwise a new record is read from DATA and the DO WHILE continues.

Notice that although the tape input and disk output files are record, the printer is stream. This demonstrates that record and stream I/O may be used in the same program. However at no time can record and stream be used for the same file.

Reading an Indexed Sequential File Directly

Direct access of an indexed sequential file may be required when a small number of inquiries are made about particular records on the file. Using the direct approach, only the records desired are accessed. This results in considerable time saving since most records in the file are not read.

Using the file just created in Fig. 10-3, let us write a program to read a number of data cards which request print-out of certain subscriber's records. Since each card requests an individual record, the sequence of data is not important.

This program also requires a new form of I/O statement for direct access. The general format is shown in Fig. 10-4.

---

1 2

READ FILE(*filename*) INTØ(*structure*) KEY(*expression*);

Fig. 10-4

This READ statement reads the file specified and searches, via the index, for a record which contains a key equal to the expression in the KEY clause. The equal record is placed into the structure specified. If an equal is not found, a KEY condition is raised. The following example shows how this READ is used.

READ FILE(MASTER) INTØ(RECØRD) KEY(A);

If A had been previously assigned a value of 375, the MASTER file would be examined for a record containing a Key with the value 375. This record will be placed in the structure named RECØRD.

In this program called INQUIRY we will read records from cards which supply the key of the disk record required. Records that are found on disk will be printed. Those not found, as identified by a key error, will be printed with a message "Not Found." The top down is as follows:

INQUIRY – Top Down Development

1. Open Files

2. Read initial record

3. Find and print disk records

4. Close Files

5. Stop

3. FIND

    3.1 On key error set error switch
                       print error record

    3.2 Repeat level 3.2 until end of file

        3.2.1 Read FILEI using the card key

        3.2.2 If no key error move the record found to print area
                       and print
                       else turn error switch off

        3.2.3 Read next card

In the program in Fig. 10–5 the indexed sequential file FILEI is declared as a DIRECT INPUT file. Each record read from CARD supplies a key which is used in the READ for FILEI to access the desired record directly. This record is then assigned to the elements of PREC1 prior to calling PRINT.

A key error in this program is the result of not finding a record in FILEI with the required key. In this case a message 'NØT FØUND' is printed.

```
01  INQUIRY: PROC OPTIONS(MAIN);
02  DCL CARD RECORD INPUT ENV(MEDIUM(SYSIPT,2501)F
        BLKSIZE(80)),
        REPORT RECORD OUTPUT ENV(MEDIUM(SYSLST,1403) F
            BLKSIZE(133) CTLASA);
03  DCL FILEI RECORD INPUT DIRECT KEYED ENV(MEDIUM(SYS000,
        3340) F BLKSIZE(50) INDEXED KEYLENGTH(4)
        EXTENTNUMBER(3) OFLTRACKS(1)));
04  DCL KEYERROR FIXED(1) INIT(0);
05  DCL 1 CREC,
        2 CSUB PIC'(4)X',
        2 CFILL PIC'(76)X';
06  DCL 1 SREC,
        2 SSUB PIC'(4)X',
```

```
              2 SCODE PIC '9',
              2 SNAME PIC'(19)X',
              2 SADDRESS PIC'(20)X',
              2 SDATE PIC'(6)9';
07   DCL 1 PREC1,
              2 PCTL PIC'X',
              2 PSUB PIC'(4)X',
              2 P1 PIC'XX',
              2 PNAME PIC'(19)X',
              2 PADDRESS PIC'(20)X',
              2 P3 PIC'XX',
              2 PDATE PIC'99B99B99',
              2 P4 PIC'(77)X';
08   DCL 1 PREC2 DEF PREC1,
              2 P5 PIC'(133)X';
09   I=0;    /* ENDFILE SWITCH */
10   P5=' ';    /* CLEAR PRINT AREA */
11   OPEN FILE(CARD), FILE(REPORT), FILE(FILEI);
12   ON ENDFILE(SYSIN) I=1;
13   READ FILE(CARD) INTO(CREC);
14   CALL FIND;
15   CLOSE FILE(CARD), FILE(REPORT), FILE(FILEI);
16   STOP;
17   FIND:PROC;
18      ON KEY(FILEI) BEGIN;    /* NO RECORD ON FILE I */
19         KEYERROR=1;
20         PSUB=CSUB;
21         P4='NOT FOUND';
22         CALL PRINT;
23         END;
24      DO WHILE(I=0);
25       READ FILE(FILEI) INTO (SREC) KEY(CSUB);
26        IF KEYERROR = 0 THEN DO;    /* RECORD FOUND */
27         PSUB=SSUB;
28         PNAME=SNAME;
29         PADDRESS=SADDRESS;
30         PDATE=SDATE;
31         CALL PRINT;
32         END;
33         ELSE KEYERROR=0;             /* RECORD NOT FOUND */
34        READ FILE(CARD) INTO(CREC);
35        END;
36   END FIND;
37   PRINT:PROC;
```

```
38  PCTL='0';
39  WRITE FILE(REPORT) FROM(PREC1);
40  P5=' ';    /* CLEAR PRINT LINE */
41  END PRINT;
42  END INQUIRY;
```

Fig. 10-5

An endfile on CARD indicates no additional requests are to be made and the program is terminated.

Reading an Indexed Sequential File Sequentially

The same file that was accessed directly in Fig. 10-5 may also be read sequentially. The approach taken is similar to reading a sequential file.

The major difference in dealing with an indexed sequential file is positioning to the first record in the file. This can be done by issuing a direct read using the key of the first record. We know this key because we created a record with a key of zeroes in Fig. 10-3. Subsequent records are then read as usual for a sequential file. The following is the top down development for the sequential reading of an indexed file.

SEQ - Top Down Development

1. Open Files

2. Read first dummy record

3. Read initial record

4. Repeat until no more records

      4.1 Move data to print area

      4.2 Print

      4.3 Read next record

5. Close Files

6. Stop

Figure 10-6 shows the PL/I program for this application. The internal procedure PRINT is used to simply print a line for each record read from FILEI except for the dummy record. This could of course be expanded to create headings, page overflow, and so on as need demands.

```
01   SEQ: PROC OPTIONS(MAIN);
02   DCL FILEI RECORD INPUT KEYED ENV(MEDIUM(SYS000,3340)
               F BLKSIZE(50) INDEXED KEYLENGTH(4)
               EXTENTNUMBER(3) OFLTRACKS(1));
03   DCL 1 SREC,
             2 SSUB PIC'(4)X',
             2 SCODE PIC '9',
             2 SNAME PIC'(19)X',
             2 SADDRESS PIC'(20)X',
             2 SDATE PIC'(6)9';
04   DCL REPORT RECORD OUTPUT ENV(MEDIUM(SYSLST,1403)
             F BLKSIZE(133) CTLASA);
05   DCL 1 PREC1,
             2 PCTL PIC'X',
             2 PSUB PIC'(4)X',
             2 P1 PIC'XX',
             2 PNAME PIC'(19)X',
             2 PADDRESS PIC'(20)X',
             2 P3 PIC'XX',
             2 PDATE PIC'99B99B99',
             2 P4 PIC'(77)X';
06   DCL 1 PREC2 DEF PREC1,
             2 P5 PIC'(133)X';
07   I=0;      /* ENDFILE SWITCH */
08   P5=' ';      /* CLEAR PRINT AREA */
09   OPEN FILE(REPORT), FILE(FILEI);
10   ON ENDFILE(FILEI) I=1;
                       /* POSITION TO START OF FILE */
11   READ FILE(FILEI) INTO(SREC) KEY('0000');
                       /* READ INITIAL RECORD */
12   READ FILE(FILEI) INTO(SREC);
13   DO WHILE(I=0);
14      PSUB=SSUB;
15      PNAME=SNAME;
16      PADDRESS=SADDRESS;
17      PDATE=SDATE;
18      CALL PRINT;
19      READ FILE(FILEI) INTO(SREC);
20      END;
21   CLOSE FILE(FILEI), FILE(REPORT);
22   STOP;
23   PRINT:PROC;
24   PCTL='0';
```

```
25  WRITE FILE(REPORT) FROM(PREC1);
26  P5=' ';      /* CLEAR PRINT LINE */
27  END PRINT;
28  END SEQ;
```

Fig. 10–6

In this program no ØN KEY statement has been used since we have a master file without errors. If, in fact, a key error occurred in this program the program would automatically terminate. This is desirable since a major problem would have occurred in this file which is beyond the capability of this program to correct.

Since this file is being processed sequentially, the ØN ENDFILE is used in the same way as for any other sequential file.

Updating an Indexed Sequential File

An update program for an indexed sequential file differs from a sequential file in two major ways:

1. Transactions are not necessarily in sequence.

2. The updated master file is the same file as the original master except for revisions which have been made. There is not a separate output master file as there was for a sequential update (see Chapter 9).

Rewrite

In writing the update, the REWRITE statement is needed. The general format is shown in Fig. 10–7.

```
1 2

  REWRITE FILE(filename) FRØM(structure)
     KEY(expression);
```

Fig. 10–7

The REWRITE is used when a record has been previously read from an indexed sequential file. Usually the record has been updated or revised in some way and the new version of the record is to be placed on the DASD in the original location. An example of the REWRITE might be as follows:

REWRITE FILE(DISK) FRØM(RECØRD) KEY(PART);

This statement takes the data found in the structure named RECØRD and, using the key called PART, writes the record onto the file DISK into the location which contains an equal key. The data which originally occupied the location with the equal key is replaced by the data found in RECØRD.

Figure 10-8 shows the update program for the indexed sequential file. Transactions are on tape in the following format:

1-4	Subscription Number		
5	Record Code	1	New Record
		2	Revision
		3	Deletion
6-24	Subscriber's Name		
25-44	Subscriber's Address		
45-50	Date of Final Issue		

UPDATE – Top Down Development

1. Open Files

2. Read initial transaction

3. Repeat until no more transactions

    3.1 If code 1 then process new records

    3.2 If code 2 then process revise records

    3.3 If code 3 then process deletions

    3.4 Read next transaction

4. Close Files

5. Stop

Procedures

6. NEW

    6.1 On key error print 'equal record found' message

    6.2 Move data to the new record

    6.3 Write on FILEI

7. REVISE

    7.1 On key error print 'no record to revise' message

    7.2 Read FILEI

    7.3 If record is found change the address
                     Rewrite the record on FILEI

8. DELETE

    8.1 On key error print 'no record to delete' message

    8.2 Read FILEI

    8.3 If record is found enter a delete code
                     Rewrite the record on FILEI

```
1  UPDATE:PROC OPTIONS(MAIN);
2  DCL CARD RECORD INPUT ENV(MEDIUM(SYSIPT,2501)F
        BLKSIZE(80)),
        REPORT RECORD OUTPUT ENV(MEDIUM(SYSLST,1403)F
            BLKSIZE(133) CTLASA);
3  DCL FILEI RECORD UPDATE DIRECT KEYED ENV(MEDIUM(SYS000,
        3340) F BLKSIZE(50) INDEXED KEYLENGTH(4)
        EXTENTNUMBER(3) OFLTRACKS(1));
4  DCL KEYERROR FIXED(1) INIT(0);
5  DCL 1 CREC,      /* CARD INPUT STRUCTURE */
        2 CSUB PIC'(4)X',
        2 CCODE PIC'9',
        2 CNAME PIC'(19)X',
        2 CADR PIC'(20)X',
        2 CDATE PIC'(6)X',
        2 CFILL PIC'(30)X';
6  DCL 1 SREC,      /* SUBSCRIBER MASTER INPUT */
        2 SSUB PIC'(4)X',
        2 SCODE PIC '9',
        2 SNAME PIC'(19)X',
        2 SADDRESS PIC'(20)X',
        2 SDATE PIC'(6)9';
7  DCL 1 PREC1,      /* PRINTER OUTPUT */
        2 PCTL PIC'X',
        2 PSUB PIC'(4)X',
        2 P1 PIC'XX',
        2 PNAME PIC'(19)X',
        2 PADDRESS PIC'(20)X',
        2 P3 PIC'XX',
        2 PDATE PIC'99B99B99',
        2 P4 PIC'(77)X';
```

```
 8  DCL 1 PREC2 DEF PREC1,
         2 P5 PIC'(133)X';
 9  I=0;      /* ENDFILE SWITCH */
10  P5=' ';      /* CLEAR PRINT AREA */
11  OPEN FILE(CARD), FILE(REPORT), FILE(FILEI);
12  ON ENDFILE(SYSIN) I=1;
13  READ FILE(CARD) INTO(CREC);
14  DO WHILE (I=0);
15      IF CCODE=1 THEN CALL NEW;
16      ELSE IF CCODE=2 THEN CALL REVISE;
17      ELSE IF CCODE=3 THEN CALL DELETE;
18      READ FILE(CARD) INTO(CREC);
19      END;
20  CLOSE FILE(CARD), FILE(REPORT), FILE(FILEI);
21  STOP;
22  NEW:PROC;      /* CREATE NEW MASTER */
23  ON KEY(FILEI) BEGIN;
24      PCTL='0';
25      PSUB=CSUB;
26      PNAME='EQUAL RECORD FOUND';
27      CALL PRINT;
28      END;
29  SSUB=CSUB;
30  SCODE=CCODE;
31  SADDRESS=CADR;
32  SDATE=CDATE;
33  WRITE FILE(FILEI) FROM(SREC) KEYFROM(SSUB);
34  END NEW;
35  REVISE: PROC;      /* CHANGE OF ADDRESS */
36  ON KEY(FILEI) BEGIN;
37      PCTL='0';
38      PSUB=CSUB;
39      PNAME='NO RECORD TO REVISE';
40      CALL PRINT;
41      KEYERROR=1;
42      END;
43  READ FILE(FILEI) INTO(SREC) KEY(CSUB);
44  IF KEYERROR=0 THEN DO;
45      SADDRESS=CADR;      /* CHANGE ADDRESS */
46      REWRITE FILE(FILEI) FROM(SREC) KEY(CSUB);
47      END;
48      ELSE KEYERROR=0;
49  END REVISE;
```

```
50  DELETE:PROC;     /* DELETE MASTER */
51  ON KEY(FILEI) BEGIN;
52      PCTL='0';
53      PSUB=CSUB;
54      PNAME='NO RECORD TO DELETE';
55      CALL PRINT;
56      KEYERROR=1;
57      END;
58  READ FILE(FILEI) INTO(SREC) KEY(CSUB);
59  IF KEYERROR=0 THEN DO;
60      SCODE=3;     /* CODE RECORD AS DELETED */
61      REWRITE FILE(FILEI) FROM(SREC) KEY(CSUB);
62      END;
63      ELSE KEYERROR=0;
64  END DELETE;
65  PRINT:PROC;
66  WRITE FILE(REPORT)FROM(PREC1);
67  P5=' ';
68  END PRINT;
69  END UPDATE;
```

Fig. 10-8

The update program assumes that all transactions on tape have been previously edited and they do not contain coding errors. That is, each field is recorded correctly and any transactions with invalid fields would not have been included in this file.

The main line of the program consists primarily of a READ statement and a series of IF statements to determine the type of updating to be done. Three internal procedures are then used to process the three types of transactions.

In NEW procedure, a WRITE is issued to write the new record on the file. This action causes the computer to find an available location for the record on the DASD and store it there. If an equal record already exists on the file, a key error results and a message is written on the printer.

In REVISE, a direct read is used, supplying the key of the record desired. If an equal record is found it is placed in S_REC. The address field is then updated. The revised record is then rewritten on the DASD.

In the event that a key error occurs, this indicates that the file does not contain the desired record. A message to this effect is printed.

DELETE is the only unobvious procedure. With indexed sequential files there is no way to physically remove the record from the file during an update run. Instead a code is written on the record to indicate a deletion.

It is quite probable that the file would at all times have some records coded as being deleted. These could be used by releasing the subscription number to a new customer. How the program logic would handle this is left up to the reader as a programming exercise.

Deleted records may also be removed completely by doing a sequential read of the file as input. Another indexed sequential output file is created and any record containing a deletion code would simply not be written on the newly created file. This type of program would be run rather infrequently, usually when the number of deleted records increased above a certain predetermined maximum.

Programming Problems

1. An automobile insurance company retains all of its policyholder's records on an indexed sequential 2314 DASD in the following format:

1- 7	Policy Number
10-25	Customer's Name
26-50	Customer's Address
51-52	Year of Automobile
53-62	Make of Automobile
63-75	Serial Number
80-85	Effective Date
86-91	Expiration Date
92-100	Rating Codes (1 byte per code)
101-104	Unused

    Inquiries are to be made to this file by submitting the desired policy number in columns 1-7 of a data card. Access of the file is to be direct. Equal records found are to be printed, one per page, showing all of the information contained in file. When a record is not found an appropriate message should be printed.

2. A manufacturing firm retains a record of all assembly operations on an indexed sequential 2311 DASD in the following format:

1- 4	Assembly Number
5- 9	Number of Units Assembled (One decimal)
10-15	Number of Hours in Assembly (One decimal)
16	Unused

    As each employee completes work on a given assembly, the number of units completed (or fraction thereof) and the amount of time spent on the assembly is recorded on a card in the following format:

1- 4	Assembly Number
5- 7	Department Number
8-12	Employee Number
13-16	Number of Units Assembled (One decimal)
17-19	Number of Hours in Assembly (One decimal)
20-80	Unused

Each card submitted is used to directly update the above file. The number of units and hours are added to the respective fields in the master file.

If an equal record cannot be found a message to that effect, including all card data, is written on the printer.

In addition each card record successfully processed is written on tape. This provides a backup record of all data affecting the master file. Use record I/O for all files in this program.

3. An airline reservation system contains an indexed sequential file in the following format:

1	Deletion Code	
2- 4	Flight Number	
5	Flight Code	1 – Departing
		0 – Arriving
6- 8	Destination or Arrived From Code	
9-12	Time of Departure or Arrival	
13-14	Number of First Class Passengers	
15-16	Capacity for First Class Passengers	
17-19	Number of Economy Passengers	
20-22	Capacity for Economy Passengers	
23-32	Unused	

Reservations are recorded in the system with a record of the following format:

1	Code – E – Economy Reservation	
	F – First Class Reservation	
2-4	Flight Number	
5	Cancellation – C	
	– Otherwise blank	

Each reservation causes one to be added to either first class or economy and a printout advising that the reservation has been made. When the number reaches the capacity recorded a second message is printed advising that no additional reservations may be made in that section.

A cancellation will reduce the number of passengers by one.

In addition a new flight may be set up on the file, or a revision to an existing flight, with the following record:

1	Code N – New Flight
	R – Revision
2– 4	Flight Number
5	Flight Code
6– 8	Destination or Arrived From Code
9–12	Time of Departure or Arrival
15–16	Capacity for First Class
20–22	Capacity for Economy

All information is recorded in the new record with the number of passengers initially set to zero. It is likely that some flight numbers will be reused. In this case the deletion code in the master would contain a "1." This indicates that the record is not presently in use but may be reactivated. When this is done, set deletion code to blank.

A revision merely changes those fields recorded in the transaction record. Blank fields require no revision.

4. An interesting addition to the program of problem 3 involves the use of an alternate flight number in positions 24–26 in the master file. If this flight is filled to capacity the alternate flight is searched for available seats. An alternate flight may itself have another alternate flight if applicable. When there is no other alternate flight, this field (24–26) will contain zeroes.

Miscellaneous Statements

In this chapter, additional PL/I statements are reviewed with the intention of making the reader aware of their availability. They are the type of statements which are unlikely to be used in every program but on occasion will be found useful.

On Conditions

In Chapter 5, the ØN ENDFILE statement was discussed and in Chapter 10 the ØN KEY was used. The following are additional ØN statements which function in a similar way to these statements.

Input or Output Conditions

The first group of ØN conditions relates to errors or conditions which may occur during an input or an output operation.

ENDPAGE

This condition is used only for stream output printer files. It must be associated with a filename which is the name of the file being written by the PUT LIST or PUT EDIT statement.

As printing occurs, the system is testing for the end of page condition.

When the end of the page is reached, the ØN ENDPAGE condition will be executed. The general format is shown in Fig. 11-1.

1| 2

    ØN ENDPAGE *(filename) action;*

Fig. 11-1

ØN ENDPAGE   Are keywords specifying the condition to be
                                    tested.

(filename)   Is the name of the file for the specified con-
                                    dition.

action   Specifies the action to be taken when the
                                    condition occurs.

    An example of this is as follows:

    ØN ENDPAGE(PRINT) BEGIN;
       CALL HEAD;
       END;

    In this statement, when an end of page is reached on file, PRINT control in the program will branch to procedure HEAD. HEAD would be written to cause a skip to a new page and print the heading on that page.

Record

    This condition may be used for record-oriented files. It is also associated with a filename which specifies the file to which this condition pertains.

    As a file is being either read or written, with a READ, REWRITE, or LØ-CATE statement, the record length is being checked to ensure that it corresponds with the length of the structure which relates to the input or output operation. If the length of the record is not the same as the length of the structure, then the RECØRD condition is raised. The general format is shown in Fig. 11-2.

1| 2

    ØN RECØRD *(filename) action;*

Fig. 11-2

ØN RECØRD   Are keywords specifying the condition to be
                                       tested.

(*filename*)   Is the name of the file tested for the speci-
                                       fied condition.

action   Specifies the action to be taken when a rec-
                                       ord error occurs.

An example of this statement might be

ØN RECØRD(FILEA) CALL ERRØR_A;

In this case when a record length error occurs on FILEA control will
branch to a procedure named ERRØR_A. This routine would likely print an
error message.

The advantage with this statement is that the programmer retains control
of the processing. The record may be ignored if desired, or an attempt made to
process it if this is deemed advisable. Without ØN RECØRD this type of error
would automatically terminate the program, but with this ØN condition the programmer retains control.

Another use of the ØN RECØRD allows for a null action. This is written
as follows:

ØN RECØRD (FILEA);

This specifies that a record condition is to be tested on FILEA but if
found, no action is to be taken. Processing proceeds normally even though the
record is of an incorrect length. This approach may be useful when dealing with
a file which intentionally contains records of varying length.

Computational Conditions

This group of ØN conditions relates to errors occurring during a computational
operation such as evaluating an arithmetic expression.

Conversion

This condition relates to stream files and the data in these files. It also relates to internal computations. You will recall that when a punched card contains numeric data, the format item used in a GET EDIT is of the form $F(l,d)$
and that for this field a DECIMAL FIXED variable would be declared. Recall
that this variable will be stored internally in packed decimal form (see Chapter
9). If the card field contains other than numerical information, a conversion
error will occur. This condition relates to any attempted conversion which is in-

valid. See Appendix B for a chart of valid conversions. The general format is shown in Fig. 11-3.

1	2
	ØN CØNVERSIØN *action;*

Fig. 11-3

ØN CØNVERSIØN   Are the keywords specifying the condition to be tested.

action   This specifies the action to be taken when the error occurs.

Even though an I/O operation may be involved, the conversion error relates to internal conversions on data. Thus no filename is used. An example may be shown simply by

ØN CØNVERSIØN BEGIN;

When a conversion error occurs, the BEGIN block will be executed.

Fixedoverflow

This condition relates to DECIMAL FIXED or BINARY FIXED arithmetic operations. It occurs whenever the result of the operation exceeds the limit for the length of these variables. As indicated in Chapter 3, the maximum length for DECIMAL FIXED is 15 and for BINARY FIXED 31. The general format is shown in Fig. 11-4.

1	2
	ØN FIXEDØVERFLØW *action;*

Fig. 11-4

ØN FIXEDØVERFLØW   Are keywords specifying the condition to be tested.

action   This is taken when the condition occurs.

As for other ØN conditions, the FIXEDØVERFLØW allows the programmer to retain control of the program when this condition occurs. An example is

ØN FIXEDØVERFLØW CALL F_ERR;

When a fixed overflow occurs in the program, control branches to a routine labelled F_ERR.

Overflow

This condition is identical to FIXEDØVERFLØW except that it relates to DECIMAL FLØAT with a maximum of 10^{75} and to BINARY FLØAT with a maximum of 2^{252}. The general format is shown in Fig. 11-5.

```
1 2

    ØN ØVERFLØW action;
```

Fig. 11-5

ØN ØVERFLØW   Keywords specifying condition to be tested.
                               Follow by the action taken.

Underflow

The underflow condition is similar to the overflow except that it occurs when the value of a DECIMAL FLØAT or BINARY FLØAT number becomes smaller than the minimum size permitted. For DECIMAL FLØAT this is 10^{-78} and for BINARY FLØAT it is 2^{-260}. The general format is shown in Fig. 11-6.

```
1 2

    ØN UNDERFLØW action;
```

Fig. 11-6

Zerodivide

This condition occurs whenever an attempt is made by the program to divide by zero. This applies to both fixed and float variables. The general format is shown in Fig. 11-7.

1	2
	ØN ZERØDIVIDE *action;*

Fig. 11-7

Whenever a division by zero is attempted in PL/I the result is undefined. This means we have no way of determining what the result will be. This of course could result in further difficulties, such as a conversion error, later in the program. The zero divide condition helps in detecting this error and taking appropriate action before other errors might occur.

Signal

This is not an ØN condition but is a useful tool for testing ØN conditions used in the program. The general format is shown in Fig. 11-8.

1	2
	SIGNAL *name of condition;*

Fig. 11-8

SIGNAL   Is a keyword which specifies that a certain
                                condition is to be simulated.

name of condition   Is the condition which is to be simulated.

Suppose we have a program which tests for a CØNVERSION condition. We know that ultimately a conversion error will occur but that our present data does not actually have anything which would cause a conversion error. SIGNAL may be used to test this ØN condition without actually encountering the condition itself. The following statements show how:

```
A:PRØC;
    ØN CØNVERSIØN BEGIN;
        .
    END;
        .
    X = X * ((Y + 7.9)/B(K));
```

SIGNAL CØNVERSIØN;

.

.

.

.

.

.

END A;

Here the ØN CØNVERSIØN causes the program to execute error statements in the BEGIN block. This happens when the SIGNAL statement is
encountered in the program. This effectively simulates the occurrence of a
conversion error in the arithmetic expression.

Built-In Functions

In Chapter 4 some commonly used built-in functions (SQRT,SIN,CØS) were
discussed. In this section some other useful functions available in PL/I will be
examined. They are organized into three categories: mathematical, arithmetic,
and string.

Mathematical Functions

All mathematical functions described here have the same general format as
shown below.

function name (e)

function name	The name of the function as specified in the following discussion.
(e)	The expression, variable or constant, to be evaluated by the function.

Mathematical functions are normally used in assignment statements or
arithmetic expressions. This was discussed in detail in Chapter 4. Briefly the following examples show how the sine function was applied.

$$X = SIN(A);$$
$$X = SIN(A+B);$$
$$Y = A*(1 + SIN(B));$$

COSD

This function finds the cosine of a given value which is expressed in degrees. This differs from CØS which requires a value in radians. An example of CØSD is

$$A = CØSD(45);$$

This would return the cosine of $45°$ which is approximately .70711 to the variable A. The precision of the result depends upon the precision of the variable A.

SIND

Like CØSD this function finds the sine of a given value which is expressed in degrees. Thus the expression

$$B = SIND(Q);$$

takes the present value of Q, which must represent degrees, determines its sine, and assigns this result to B.

TAN

TAN is a function which finds the tangent of variable which is in radians. This may be expressed as follows:

$$T = TAN(A * B);$$

This statement determines the product of A and B which represents radians, finds the tangent of this product, and assigns the tangent to the variable T.

TAND

TAND is a function which finds the tangent of a variable which is expressed in degrees. If the statement used in this case was

$$T = TAND(A * B);$$

then A and B must be variables which represent degrees. The resulting action would be the same as for the previous example.

LOG

This function finds the natural logarithm which is taken to the base *e* of a specified value. This may be expressed as follows:

$$W = L\emptyset G(X);$$

which finds the natural logarithm of the variable X and assigns it to W.

LOG10

L∅G10 is similar to L∅G except that it finds the common logarithm which is taken to base 10 of a given variable. This is demonstrated by the expression

$$S = 1 + L\emptyset G10(A);$$

which finds the common logarithm of A, adds the constant 1 to it and assigns the result to S.

LOG2

This function is also similar to L∅G except that it finds the binary logarithm which is taken to base 2 of a specified variable. Thus the statement

$$B = L\emptyset G2(10);$$

finds the binary logarithm of the decimal value 10 and assigns it to B.

Arithmetic Functions

Some of the more useful arithmetic functions are discussed here. Since each format varies depending upon the function used, a general format is given separately with each function described.

ABS

This function finds the absolute value of an expression, variable, or constant. The general format is

$$ABS(e)$$

This is demonstrated by the statements

$$N = ABS(75);$$
$$N = ABS(-75);$$

In either case N receives the value 75 since this is the absolute value of either expression.

MAX

This function finds the highest value of a series of two or more expressions, variables or constants. The general format is

$$MAX\ (e_1, e_2, \ldots, e_n)$$

An example of this is shown by the statements

$$A = 1.4;$$
$$B = 3.0;$$
$$W = MAX((2*A)\ ,\ 3.1\ ,\ B);$$

In this statement W would receive the value 3.1 since it is greater than $(2*A)$ which evaluates to 2.8 and it is also greater than B.

MIN

This function is similar to MAX except that it finds the minimum value of a series of two or more arguments. The general format is

$$MIN\ (e_1, e_2, \ldots, e_n)$$

An example using MIN to find LOWTAG when using the Balance Line Method in Chapter 9 is

$$LØWTAG = MIN(MSTØCK,TSTØCK);$$

The MIN function would find the lowest of MSTØCK or TSTØCK and assign this value to LØWTAG.

ROUND

This function takes a variable which contains a fractional part and rounds it at a specified digit. The general format for RØUND is

$$RØUND(e,d)$$

where e is the expression or value to be rounded and d is the digit at which rounding is to occur. This may be seen in the following example:

$$A = 23.167;$$
$$B = RØUND(A,2);$$

This causes the value in A to be rounded at the second digit to the right of the decimal point. Thus B receives the value 23.17. If the statements had been

$$A = 23.1671;$$
$$B = R\emptyset UND(A,3);$$

the result in B would be 23.167.

String Functions

The string functions are used for manipulating character or bit string data. Again, since each general format is unique they will be discussed independently.

CHAR

The CHAR built-in function is used to convert a given value to a character string. This function would be used when the normal conversion of data is impossible. The general format is

$$CHAR(e)$$

where CHAR is the name of the function and e represents the expression, variable, or constant to be converted to a character string.

We might want to print a picture using a PUT LIST. However, some compilers don't permit this. Figure 11-9 shows how this may be done.

```
DCL X PIC'$$$,$$9V.99',
    Y CHAR (10),
    Z FIXED (7,2);
GET LIST (Z);
    .
    .
    .

X = Z;
Y = CHAR (X);
PUT LIST (Y);
```

Fig. 11-9

The picture field X is assigned to Y using the built-in function CHAR which converts it to a character string. The string Y may then be used directly in the PUT LIST.

Fig. 11-10 shows the same problem resolved more directly by using the CHAR function in the PUT LIST itself.

```
DCL X PIC '$$$,$$9V.99',
    Z FIXED (7,2);
GET LIST (Z);
    .
    .
    .

X = Z;
PUT LIST (CHAR(X));
```

Fig. 11-10

In this example the PUT LIST prints the character string which is the result of converting the picture variable X to a character string.

HIGH

This function creates a character string consisting of characters of the highest value permissible in the computer used. In System/370 this value would be hexadecimal FF (see Appendix E). The general format for HIGH is

HIGH(/)

where HIGH is the function name and (/) represents the length of the character string to be created.

The expression

FIELD = HIGH(3);

would cause three bytes of high characters (FFs) to be assigned to FIELD. It is expected that FIELD would be a character string variable.

LOW

This built-in function is similar to HIGH except that it assigns the lowest value available in the computer used. For System/370 implementation of this value would be hexadecimal 00 (see Appendix E). The general format for LØW is

LØW (/)

where LØW is the function name, and (/) represents the length of the character string to be created.

The statement

$$H\emptyset LD = L\emptyset W(5);$$

would assign five bytes of the lowest character (00s) to the variable H∅LD.

INDEX

The INDEX function may be used to search for the existence of a certain character or string of characters in a given variable. The general format for INDEX is

$$INDEX \ (v,s)$$

where INDEX is the name of the function, v represents the variable which is being searched for the desired string, and s represents the string we are looking for.

The statements in Fig. 11–11 give a simple example of how INDEX works. In this case the field A is being searched for the presence of a 3. This is found in the fifth position. Thus a binary 5 will be assigned to B. Notice that the first equal found determines the value returned. Even though there is a 3 in position 9, a 5 is returned since it is the first location a 3 is found.

```
DCL A CHAR (10),
    B BINARY FIXED (15);
A = 'XB1$3WDH3D';
B = INDEX (A, '3');
```

Fig. 11–11

If the statement had been

$$B = INDEX \ (A, \ '3D');$$

then the program will search for a configuration of a 3 followed immediately by a D. In this case the value assigned to B will be 9.

Using the statement

$$B = INDEX \ (A, \ 'E');$$

causes the value 0 to be assigned to B since no equal is found in A.

A more useful example of INDEX is shown in Fig. 11–12. In this procedure we have an array TABLE which contains 100 elements of 4 characters each. A key, which represents the value desired, is read from a data card. KEY is used in the INDEX function to search TABLE for an equal group of four characters.

When found, the result of INDEX is divided by four to give the actual subscript location of the value in the table.

```
DCL TABLE(100) CHAR(4),
    KEY CHAR(4),
    LØC FIXED(3);
    .
    .
    .

GET LIST(KEY);
LØC = (INDEX(TABLE,KEY))/4+1;
```

Fig. 11-12

SUBSTR

This function may be used to extract from a given string only certain select parts of that string. The general format is

$$SUBSTR\ (v,l,n)$$

SUBSTR	Is the function name.
v	Represents the variable from which the string is to be taken.
l	Is the location within the string.
n	Is the number of characters or bits to be extracted.

Suppose we have a variable DATE which contains day, month, and year as a character string of six characters. It is necessary to extract the month and year from DATE. The original data looks like this

DATE | 25 | 04 | 72 |

By using the statement

$$RESULT = SUBSTR\ (DATE,3,4);$$

the value in RESULT after the assignment would be

RESULT
04	72

Year itself could be extracted by using

YEAR = SUBSTR (DATE,5,2);

which will assign the 5th and 6th location of DATE to YEAR.

Other Functions

DATE

The DATE function is one of the most useful built-in functions. It operates very simply by supplying the current date to the point where it is used. The date is in the form of

YYMMDD

which is a six-byte character string where YY represents year, MM represents month, and DD represents day.

If the statement

D = DATE;

is used the current date will be assigned to the variable D. D must be a character string of length six. If the current date was March 10, 1977 then after the assign, D would contain 770310 in the form of a character string.

The BUILTIN attribute must also be used with the DATE function.

TIME

The TIME function makes the current time available to the program. This is supplied as a character string in the following form

hhmmssddd

which is a nine-byte string where *hh* represents hours in a 24-hour clock, *mm* represents minutes, *ss* seconds and *ddd* milliseconds (thousandth of a second). Thus if the statement

NØW = TIME;

were used, nine bytes of information would be assigned to NØW. If the present time was 1 PM, 17 minutes, 59 seconds and 237 milliseconds, the result in NØW would be 131759237 in the form of a character string.

TIME also requires the use of the BUILTIN attribute.

ADDR

The ADDR built-in function determines the address of a given variable and assigns this address to pointer variable. The address function provides a great deal of flexibility in programming which is not otherwise available. Its basic format is

ADDR (*e*)

where ADDR is the function name and (*e*) is the variable whose address is required.

This may be used to permit two types of data to be stored in one element of an array. Suppose we have an array TABLE where each element consists of 25 bytes. The first five bytes are a number and the other 20 a description in the form of a character string. Fig. 11-13 shows a procedure which separates these two elements.

```
DCL TABLE(100) CHAR(25);
DCL P PØINTER;
DCL 1 WØRK BASED (P),
      2 NUM PIC '(5)9',
      2 DESC PIC '(20)X';
      .
      .
      .

   P = ADDR(TABLE(I));
```

Fig. 11-13

In the assignment statement the pointer variable P is assigned the address of a given element of TABLE. The variable I, which must be previously given a value, determines the element whose address is given. Since WØRK is a structure based on the pointer P, WØRK is actually pointing to the element of the array that we require. Therefore, by referring to the variable names NUM and DESC we are actually referring directly to the two sections of the element of the array subscripted by I. Figure 11-14 shows this referencing:

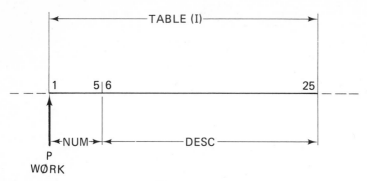

Fig. 11-14

Thus TABLE(I) consists of 25 bytes. P is pointing to the first byte of TABLE(I). Therefore, WØRK also references this first byte. NUM references bytes 1-5 within this area and DESC includes bytes 6-25 within TABLE (I).

BUILTIN ATTRIBUTE

The BUILTIN attribute is used in a declare statement to indicate that a given name is the name of a built-in function. This avoids the possible conflict between a variable name and a function name.

Suppose we are using the DATE built-in function in a program. Then the BUILTIN attribute would be used as shown in Fig. 11-15.

```
DCL DATE BUILTIN;
DCL DATEA CHAR(6);
    .
    .
    .

DATEA = DATE;
    .
    .
    .
```

Fig. 11-15

In this example the first declare describes DATE as being built-in function. The second declare sets up a six-byte character string called DATEA. In the body of the procedure an assignment statement gives DATEA the current date.

Keywords and
Abbreviations

Keywords are words used in PL/I to denote special meaning such as a built-in function or a declare attribute. Normally keywords in PL/I are not reserved words but are recognized by the context in which they are used. Keywords, however, are reserved for PL/C. See Appendix G for a list of these. Thus if we use

$$C\emptyset S = A + B;$$

the context determines that $C\emptyset S$ is in this case a variable name. However

$$X = C\emptyset S(A);$$

indicates that the cosine function is being used. An exception to this is when $C\emptyset S$ is declared as a one-dimensional array. Then this statement refers to position A in the array.

To avoid confusion it is best to use keywords for their intended purpose. However, the flexibility is available if the programmer feels it is justified.

KEYWORD	USE
ABS(e)	absolute function
ADDR(e)	address function
AUT$\emptyset$MATIC	declare attribute
BASED(p)	declare attribute

KEYWORD	USE
BEGIN	statement
BINARY	declare attribute
BIT	declare attribute
BUFFERED	declare attribute
BUILTIN	declare attribute
BY	DØ statement
CALL	statement
CHAR(*e*)	character function
CHARACTER	declare attribute
CLØSE	statement
CØLUMN(*p*)	format item
CØS(*e*)	cosine function
CØSD(*e*)	cosine function
DATE	date function
DECIMAL	declare attribute
DECLARE	statement
DEFINED	statement
DIRECT	statement
DØ	statement
EDIT	stream I/O
ELSE	part of IF statement
END	statement
ENDFILE	condition
ENDPAGE	condition
ENVIRØNMENT	declare attribute
EXTERNAL	declare attribute
FILE	declare attribute
FIXED	declare attribute
FIXEDØVERFLØW	condition
FLØAT	declare attribute
FØRMAT	statement
FRØM	WRITE or REWRITE statement
GET	statement
GØ TØ	statement
HIGH(*n*)	high value function
IF	statement
INDEX (*v,s*)	index function
INITIAL	declare attribute
INPUT	declare attribute
INTERNAL	declare attribute
INTØ	READ statement

KEYWORD	USE
KEY	used in READ or REWRITE
KEYED	declare attribute
KEYFRØM	used in WRITE or LØCATE
LABEL	declare attribute
LINE	format item
LIST	stream I/O
LØCATE	statement
LØG	logarithm function
LØG2	logarithm function
LØG10	logarithm function
LØW(*n*)	low value function
MAIN	procedure option
MAX	maximum function
MIN	minimum function
ØN	statement
ØPEN	statement
ØPTIØNS	procedure option
ØVERFLOW	condition
PAGE	format item
PICTURE	declare attribute
PØINTER	declare attribute
PRINT	declare attribute
PRØCEDURE	statement
PUT	statement
READ	statement
RECØRD	declare attribute
RETURN	statement
REWRITE	statement
RØUND	function
SET	READ and LØCATE option
SIGNAL	statement
SIN(*e*)	sine function
SIND(*e*)	sine function
SKIP	format item
SQRT(*e*)	square root function
STATIC	declare attribute
STØP	statement
STREAM	declare attribute
STRING	GET and PUT option
SUBSTR(*v,l,n*)	sub-string function
TAN(*e*)	tangent function

KEYWORD	USE
TAND(*e*)	tangent function
THEN	used in IF statement
TIME	time function
TØ	used in DØ statement
UPDATE	declare attribute
WHILE	option in DØ statement
WRITE	statement
ZERØDIVIDE	condition

KEYWORD	ABBREVIATION
BINARY	BIN
CHARACTER	CHAR
DECIMAL	DEC
DECLARE	DCL
DEFINED	DEF
ENVIRØNMENT	ENV
EXTERNAL	EXT
INITIAL	INIT
PICTURE	PIC
POINTER	PTR
PROCEDURE	PROC

Conversions

FROM \ TO	DECIMAL FIXED	PICTURE NUMERIC	DECIMAL FLØAT	BINARY FLØAT	BINARY FIXED	CHARACTER	BIT	LABEL	PØINTER
DECIMAL FIXED	D	C	C	C	D	NP	D	NP	NP
PICTURE NUMERIC	C	C	C	C	C	D	C	NP	NP
DECIMAL FLØAT	C	C	D	C	C	NP	C	NP	NP
BINARY FLØAT	C	C	C	C	C	D	C	NP	NP
BINARY FIXED	D	C	C	C	D	NP	D	NP	NP
CHARACTER	NP	NP	NP	NP	NP	D	C	NP	NP
BIT	D	C	D	C	D	C	D	NP	NP
LABEL	NP	NP	NP	NP	NP	NP	NP	D	NP
PØINTER	NP	NP	NP	NP	NP	NP	NP	NP	D

NP – Not Possible

D – Directly Assigned

C – Assigned via a Conversion Subroutine

C

CTLASA &
CTL360 Characters

CTLASA	CHARACTER CODES
blank	Space one line before printing
0	Space two lines before printing
−	Space three lines before printing
+	Suppress spacing
1	Skip to channel 1 before printing
2	Skip to channel 2 before printing
3	Skip to channel 3 before printing
4	Skip to channel 4 before printing
5	Skip to channel 5 before printing
6	Skip to channel 6 before printing
7	Skip to channel 7 before printing
8	Skip to channel 8 before printing
9	Skip to channel 9 before printing
A	Skip to channel 10 before printing
B	Skip to channel 11 before printing
C	Skip to channel 12 before printing
V	Select punch stacker 1
W	Select punch stacker 2

CTL360	PUNCHED CARD CODES
12,9,1	Write – no space
12,9,8,1	Write and space 1 line after printing
11,9,1	Write and space 2 lines after printing
11,9,8,1	Write and space 3 lines after printing
12,0,9	Write and skip to channel 1 after printing
12,11,1	Write and skip to channel 2 after printing
12,11,9	Write and skip to channel 3 after printing
11,0,1	Write and skip to channel 4 after printing
11,0,9	Write and skip to channel 5 after printing
12,11,0,1	Write and skip to channel 6 after printing
12,11,0,9	Write and skip to channel 7 after printing
12,1	Write and skip to channel 8 after printing
12,9	Write and skip to channel 9 after printing
11,1	Write and skip to channel 10 after printing
11,9	Write and skip to channel 11 after printing
11,0,9,2	Write and skip to channel 12 after printing
12,9,8,3	Space 1 line immediately
11,9,2	Space 2 lines immediately
11,9,8,3	Space 3 lines immediately
12,0,8,3	Skip to channel 1 immediately
12,11,3	Skip to channel 2 immediately
12,11,8,3	Skip to channel 3 immediately
11,0,3	Skip to channel 4 immediately
11,0,8,3	Skip to channel 5 immediately
12,11,0,3	Skip to channel 6 immediately
12,11,0,8,3	Skip to channel 7 immediately
12,3	Skip to channel 8 immediately
12,0,9,8,3	Skip to channel 9 immediately
11,3	Skip to channel 10 immediately
12,11,9,8,3	Skip to channel 11 immediately
0,3	Skip to channel 12 immediately
12,9,3	No operation

Flowcharting

The symbols described here are consistent with the symbols adopted by the U.S.A. Standards Institute (USASI).

Process Symbol

```
┌─────────────────┐
│  descriptive    │
│  comment        │
└─────────────────┘
```

The process block defines operations which generally cause a change in the value or location of data. For example

Flowchart Symbol   Equivalent PL/I Statement

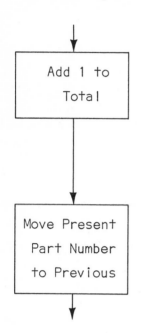

TØTAL = TØTAL + 1;

PREV_PART = PRES_PART;

INPUT/OUTPUT SYMBOL

The I/O block identifies the presence of a read or write operation. This of course refers to both stream and record I/O in PL/I.

Flowchart Symbol   Equivalent PL/I Statement

READ FILE(CARD) INTØ(RECØRD);

Flowchart Symbol   Equivalent PL/I Statement

```
PUT
 A
LINE
```
PUT LIST(A,B,C,D);

```
REWRITE
EQUAL
ACCOUNT
```
REWRITE FILE(MASTER) FRØM(REC)
KEY(ACCØUNT);

Decision Symbol

This symbol shows where a decision is made in the logic. The result of a decision may be to either two or three locations.

Flowchart Symbol   Equivalent PL/I Statement

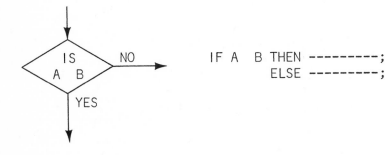

IF A   B THEN ---------;
       ELSE --------;

Flowchart Symbol   Equivalent PL/I Statement

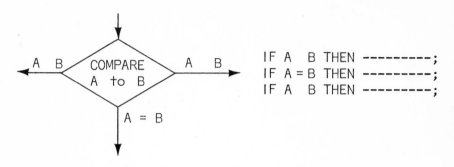

IF A   B THEN ---------;
IF A = B THEN ---------;
IF A   B THEN ---------;

Predefined Process Symbol

This symbol is used to show a procedure or function call. This indicates that a process is to be done but that the statements required are located elsewhere in the program.

Flowchart Symbol   Equivalent PL/I Statement

| Call |
| TAX |
| Procedure |

CALL TAX;

| Assign to X |
| the sine of |
| A |

X = SIN(A);

Connector Symbol

This symbol is used to show a connection to a remote part of the flowchart. It merely provides a neater way of connecting the two or more parts rather than using a lot of lines.

Terminal Symbol

This symbol is used to show where a flowchart starts, stops or exits from a procedure.

Example of a Program Flowchart

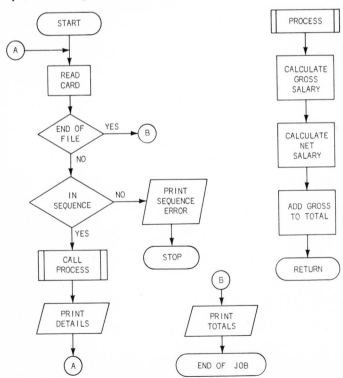

Hexadecimal Number System

The hexadecimal number system (base 16) is the system used for representing numbers in System/370. What is meant by base 16 may be more readily understood by showing how the base 10 or decimal system as we commonly know it is developed.

Given the base 10 number 1309 it is broken down into the following parts:

$$1 \times 10^3 + 3 \times 10^2 + 0 \times 10^1 + 9 \times 10^0$$

$$= 1000 + 300 + 0 + 9$$

$$= 1309_{10}$$

Ten is called the base, the numbers 3,2,1, and 0 are exponents and 1,3,0; and 9 are digits. In base 10 the highest value permitted for digits is 9. Thus numbers consist of both a digital and positional value.

In base 16 the same relationships apply. Thus the hexadecimal number 1309 may be broken down into these parts

$$1 \times 16^3 + 3 \times 16^2 + 0 \times 16^1 + 9 \times 16^0$$

$$= 4096 + 768 + 0 + 9$$

$$= 4873_{10}$$

Thus we see that 1309_{16} is equal in value to 4873_{10}. Since hexadecimal can have digital values from 0 to 15 another convention is necessary. This is due to the difficulty of representing the values 10 to 15 as digits. Therefore, the following relationships are generally used.

Hexadecimal Digit	Value
A	10
B	11
C	12
D	13
E	14
F	15

Using this notation the number $12E_{16}$ represents

$$1 \times 16^2 + 2 \times 16^1 + 14 \times 10^1 \times 16^0$$

$$= 256 + 32 + 14$$
$$= 302_{10}$$

Selected
PL/C Options

The options for PL/C programs are listed on the *PL card which precedes the main PL/C procedure statement. The general format is simply:

*PL/C options list

Each option is separated by a comma. In the following list of options, italics are used to indicate a default if the option is not used.

OPTION	DESCRIPTION
ATR, *NOATR*	Attribute Listing
ID ='name'	Program Identification. 20 characters maximum. Default prints *** NO ID ***
LINECT = n	Lines to be printed per page during compilation. Default is 60 lines.
SOURCE, NOSOURCE	Print Source Listing
XREF, *NOXREF*	Cross Reference Listing

A series of PL/C options may be entered as follows:

*PL/C ATR,ID='CASSEL',XREF

PL/C Keywords

A keyword in PL/C is an identifier which has a specific purpose. It is used to identify a particular statement type. In PL/C, keywords are reserved and may only be used for their intended purpose. They may not be used as labels or variables.

ALLOCATE	END	NO	REVERT
BEGIN	ENTRY	NOCHECK	SIGNAL
BY	EXIT	NOFLOW	SOURCE
CALL	FLOW	NOSOURCE	STOP
CHECK	FORMAT	OPEN	THEN
CLOSE	FREE	PROC	TO
DECLARE	GET	PROCEDURE	WHILE
DCL	GO	PUT	WRITE
DO	GOTO	READ	
ELSE	IF	RETURN	

Job Control Language

The following are samples of JCL cards used in various environments. Specific job control will vary from one computer installation to another. Thus it is wise to contact your computer center regarding its JCL requirements.

DOS Job Control

```
// JOB name
// OPTION LINK
// EXEC PL/I
     PL/I source program
/*
// EXEC LNKEDT
// EXEC
   data cards
/*
/&
```

DOS/VS Job Control

```
//JOB name
* $$ SLI START
// OPTION LINK,NODECK,NOLOG
   ACTION NOMAP
* $$ SLI PLI
```

     PL/I source program
/*
* $$ SLI LINK
// EXEC LNKEDT
// EXEC
    data cards
*$$ SLI END
/&

<u>PL/C Job Control</u>

  *PL/C options
     PL/C source program
  *DATA
    data cards

Index